BY GABRIELLE HAMILTON

Blood, Bones & Butter

Prune

Next of Kin

Next of Kin

Next
of
Kin

A Memoir

Gabrielle Hamilton

RANDOM HOUSE • NEW YORK

Random House
An imprint and division of Penguin Random House LLC
1745 Broadway, New York, NY 10019
randomhousebooks.com
penguinrandomhouse.com

Hardcover ISBN 978-0-399-59009-2
Ebook ISBN 978-0-399-59010-8

Printed in the United States of America on acid-free paper

1st Printing

First Edition

BOOK TEAM: Production editor: Loren Noveck • Managing editor:
Rebecca Berlant • Production manager: Richard Elman • Copy editor:
Melissa Churchill • Proofreaders: Madeline Hopkins, Mimi Lipson,
and Tess Rossi

Book design by Elizabeth Rendfleisch

The authorized representative in the EU for product safety and
compliance is Penguin Random House Ireland, Morrison Chambers,
32 Nassau Street, Dublin D02 YH68, Ireland. https://eu-contact.penguin.ie

For my boyos

Oh, but it's all right, it's all right
For we lived so well so long.

—PAUL SIMON, "AMERICAN TUNE"

CONTENTS

Part One

FACT-CHECKER

SHE LEAVES ME a message. My mother, eighty-some years old. We haven't spoken to each other in thirtyish years. Her voice is full-throated, clarion, imperious—she is ten feet tall, her footsteps set off car alarms, her teeth are as big as subway tiles, she scolds the trees, commands the rivers. But then it turns watery and apprehensive and trembly—she becomes small, made of cotton, a tucked-in child who pleads for one more story before lights-out at bedtime.

"I've just received a call from a *fact-checker* from *The New York Times Magazine* just to uh . . . whatever you've *written* in an article . . . she was checking to see if what you've *written* is *all true* . . ."

I scour the essay in my mind, wondering what I may have misstated.

"I've forgotten or I didn't *understand* what it was that you had written . . . that she had questions, that she was asking about . . . so I'm just curious to know if it was kind or *unkind* or what it was . . . but I guess I just couldn't wait to read and see it in the paper so maybe you'll let me know what it was you said, okay?"

Her water-hose voice peters out to an impotent trickle: *Was it kind, or was it unkind,* she worries.

Neither of us knows this yet, but we are about to trade places in the order of things. We are traveling toward each other from opposite ends of a long, long corridor and soon—we will brush arms as we pass—I will be the mother, she will be the child. I will find two of her teeth while sweeping the floor in her home and I will later slip one under her hospital bed pillow for tooth fairy money, I will change her smeared diaper, I will read to her, hold her face in my hands, tell her what a good girl she is being. But for now, here where this story begins, we are still the people we have always been to each other. She is still The Mother. I am still The Child. She still crisply reprimands, dismisses, criticizes; I still roil with self-recrimination.

And she has left me a voice message.

For over a decade I've written occasional features and opinion pieces for *The New York Times* but what prompts her to call after all these years concerns my monthly column, which I'd just filed: a regular ditty about food that I've been writing for the magazine for a little more than five years. I decide what I want to write about: baklava, or butter, or beans, and every month I file an 850-word essay with an accompanying well-tested recipe. This one's about a sandwich—ripe beefsteak tomatoes, sliced red onions, mayonnaise, salt, and pepper on a split baguette—that I've based on one I remember her making every day for us kids for lunch on a long-ago summer vacation in Corsica.

This sandwich was her efficient and frugal way of feeding five kids on an otherwise extravagant vacation—for which the budget had already been exhausted on airline tickets and a leased Citroën. Keeping the rest of it exceedingly, necessarily tight, she arranged rooms for us in a Catholic school dormitory vacant of students during the summer months, in exchange for a modest donation made to the convent. With only a kitchenette at the end of the hall to work with, she relied on these sandwiches as full meals, loading up the fresh, warm baguettes in the early morning and then, once tightly wrapped, stowing them in her cotton crochet sack until midday. The juicy tomatoes would soak into the bread as she marched all five of us down narrow goat paths to the black stone beaches of Ajaccio, or hiked us all up into the cool mountains above Calenzana, following a creek until she found flat, mossy rocks we could sit on for our lunch. There she would pull these hefty foot-long torpedoes from her bag and hand them out.

Everything I know about eating and cooking starts with her. She is a woman who has spent her entire indoor life in the kitchen, and her entire outdoor life in the garden or the woods; she is a woman who wakes up every day and immediately puts on her kitchen apron and ties the strings—even to read the newspaper—and only trades it in again at the very end, for her nightgown. From her I got these sandwiches, and I've duly credited her in my latest column.

When I file, they put me through the editorial procedure that they do for actual journalists. It may be only an essay about honeycomb tripe or marron glacé or—on this particular day—tomato sandwiches, but it's the paper of record, and my work gets put through four different editors, including the rigorous fact-checker.

To be fact-checked is an intimidating, thoroughgoing experience, one that I used to think was overkill for a food writer. And even though I've now been through it dozens of times— concerning such topics as peanut butter custard cake, or caviar on toast—I still feel like I am being interrogated about some wrongdoing when they request my "supporting documents" and the contact information of anyone I may have mentioned in the essay. It's as if you are a person of interest, a suspect who cannot be released until they investigate the inconsistencies in your story regarding the price you mentioned of a tub of crab meat and the price they are finding. But I send a breezy email to the assigned fact-checker with my mother's phone number and a brief heads-up before I am even asked for supporting materials—as if to declare: I'm so faithful to the truth that I *volunteer* the information before you even have a chance to ask me for it. You don't have to haul me downtown for questioning, no sir.

I email the fact-checker, *My mother is eighty-eight or eighty-nine years old—somewhere in there, I think. A little hard of hearing. Often confused by the telephone. But feel free to see what you can get from her!*

I worry that my mother, uninitiated, will be alarmed when the fact-checker calls. She has never been interviewed nor rigorously fact-checked. She lives by herself at the top of her own sylvan mountain, on her own hundred acres, with a driveway a steep and tricky quarter mile long, in the Northeast Kingdom of Vermont. For over forty years, she has lived far removed from anyone's scrutiny.

Her phone rings infrequently and only at predictable hours as she has long ago arranged it: Friends, neighbors, family, and telemarketers alike—all have received her stern instructions regarding acceptable times to disturb her with the *nuisance* of a phone call. The *New York Times* fact-checker doesn't know any of this and calls at their own convenience. I worry my mother will be set back on her heels—"Fact-checker? *The New York Times*?" You might as well say: Detective. Officer. From the FBI.

My assumption is that editors who are assigned to fact-check serious pieces of journalism are probably thick-skinned and accustomed to some level of hostility when they call their subjects, but I still feel mild concern on their behalf, should the fact-checker catch the sharp tongue of my mother's life-long insistence on proper manners and strict telephone etiquette.

What if the fact-checker behaves like one of our "weak-chinned" or "mousy" friends back when we were children in elementary school, who would call the house and whisper-squeak, "Is Gabs there?" Without the required well-mannered, full-throated preamble, "Good evening, Missus Hamilton, this is Lori calling, may I please speak with Gabrielle?"

What if the editor speaks too quickly, is on a tight deadline, is impatient to file copy, uses a cellphone and a headset for hands-free typing, and what if the connection is poor?

What if the fact-checker speaks with an accent or doesn't enunciate properly? My mother has been described by many as "a real piece of work."

Late into her eighties, she is still sharp, hale, and hardy. She drives her own car, does her own grocery shopping, cooks her own meals, weeds her garden, goes for long walks—even during the mud and the deerfly seasons—shovels snow, catches occasional mistakes on her utility bills or bank statements using a magnifying glass and calls the toll-free customer complaint lines. But she is also showing her age, a slight frailty emerges in her voice now, she is going deaf in her right ear, her memory is a steel trap here and yet cheesecloth there, and by this day, the day of the fact-checker phone call regarding a simple tomato-and-mayonnaise sandwich on a trip to Corsica one summer almost fifty years ago, she cannot always be absolutely certain what day of the month it is without first consulting her large-print calendar that she keeps by the telephone.

The telephone itself, as an instrument, and how to operate the cordless *contraption*—as she calls it when she's in a bad mood—have always been vexing, but now with advanced age, even more challenging with the added answering machine. Even in her youthful forties she could not figure out which button to push to halt the outgoing message nor which to push to retrieve the messages that pile up and beep relentlessly, demanding to be listened to, which she has more than once solved by just unplugging the thing. Even when she was younger and her hearing was practically nuclear—if not paranormal—she would direct callers to repeat themselves, to slow down, to *ar-tic-u-late,* perhaps as a means of asserting her precarious authority over a new advancing world she did not fully grasp the workings of—and in the end, she would simply prefer a postcard, a letter in the mailbox. Something she can take her time to absorb; something she can revisit without human interference or technological distractions. "Oh how I looove written correspondence!" she has always crowed. "I save every letter!"

When she moved to the Vermont mountaintop in the first place, some forty or more years ago, leaving our family home in Bucks County, Pennsylvania, amid her divorce from our father, she left behind the simple yellow rotary phone with the curlicue cord that was fastened to the wall in our kitchen, and thus had to confront, for the first time, a push-button model in her new home, which she has battled ever since, and never quite conquered. She later refused to tackle smartphones, email, USB drives, on-demand movies, file sharing, high-speed internet. And she came to rely heavily on her rural postman, for whom she leaves cookies at Christmastime in the black mailbox at the end of her driveway with a thank-you note, and with whom she has an arrangement that should he notice her mail and newspapers piling up after several days, he is to drive up the lengthy driveway and call 911 if he finds her *keeled over in her cabbages,* as she likes to put it. She spends the long Vermont nights accompanied by the Montreal classical radio station. Even while sleeping she has it playing on a transistor radio by her bed, as constant lullaby. Her overbrimming shelves of books about gardening and travel and literature and religion are kept as company, and she is surrounded by a jumbled, wild patchwork of family photographs pinned absolutely everywhere. The fact-checker must dial up and fact-check by old-fashioned landline and hope that my mother is home.

The fact-checker emails me back after the call has been accomplished:

> Your mom didn't seem to remember the sandwich. She said she thought we could trust you with the facts, though she would let me know after reading it if anything was

wrong with the piece. She asked if there was anything derogatory in it and I said no, you said her sandwich was an ideal prototype for the one you make.

I giggle a little reading this, the part where my mom says she will let the fact-checker know if I got anything wrong; thirty years spent in our separate rooms with the doors shut at opposite ends of that long corridor doesn't mean I don't recognize her instantly, doesn't mean I have misremembered who she is.

I feel tenderly toward her apparent anxiety about the possibility of there being something "derogatory" in the essay. It must be dreadful to have a writer in one's family, to have a daughter who is a writer, a daughter who may write any story she wishes, at any time, and publish it. I find myself tugged at by her worry, by her apprehensive question. There are writers who I find marvelously unconcerned with this and who say, as Anne Lamott does, *If people wanted you to write more warmly about them, they should've behaved better.* But there are other writers of magnificent discipline who adhere to a strict etiquette: *Let's wait until they are dead, and even then, don't ever speak unkindly of the dead.* And then there are the writers of universal esteem, like Lorrie Moore, who simply stick to incontrovertible Fiction.

I feel unable to commit—kind or unkind, dead or not dead, reminiscence or imagination—and I've become instead narrowly concerned with simply nailing down the verifiable details. I used to feel the facts were dull and inadequate to the writer—what are just dry facts, without the writer's poetic license to underscore and burnish their meaning? And early on, I found myself annoyed by the fact-checkers themselves, as if their diligence was deadening my vibrant prose and clumsily dulling the majesty of the Essential Truth that I meant to capture in my essays. I used to be dismissive of their overcautious, overzealous blood-hounding of the actual data. *C'mon, you want supporting documents and contact information for this essay about radishes with butter and salt?* I'd eye-roll to myself.

But it has been through them and their unrelenting fact-checking of even inconsequential material that I came to see how I had undisciplined tendencies to exaggerate what I didn't find sufficiently dramatic, and lazy impulses to elide what I didn't find convenient. I habitually brushed a few coats of saturating pigment onto whatever thing I'd describe, as if on its own, in its true and spare fact-checked dimensions, it wouldn't be credible, or, more to the point, sufficiently *incredible;* that it wouldn't leave an adequate impression on the reader. But after five years with the four separate editors who comb over even a recipe, I have come to regard the verifiable details as a place in which to relax, like a soft woven hammock tethered securely at each end between the two tall trees of It Checks Out and Your Story Squares Up, whose leaves now dapple the sunlight pleasantly on my eyelids as I doze under their protective canopy.

She thinks I can be trusted with the facts, she tells the editor.

But she wonders anxiously in her voicemail message—*I'm just curious to know if it was kind or unkind . . .* And this is followed by her heavy exhale, then her bedtime child's "Okay," and then her usual clumsy clatter to get the recalcitrant phone back into its indomitable cradle.

THE END OF AMERICAN
LITERATURE

JEFFREY DAVID HAMILTON. My oldest brother. Jeff. Jeffreaque. Jasper. J Jasper Bone. Fester. Fester von Molester. Billy. Uncle Billy. JJ. Junior. Uncle Junior. The Marquis. The Marquis of Debris. He was warm and well-mannered, introduced himself simply as Jeff Hamilton, and he was strong with eye contact and handshakes and conversations that were known to go deep quickly. Straight away you recognized him—his character—in all his many nicknames. Most prevailing, maybe, was his almost sarcastic nom de plume: JJ Bone, not even spelled out but printed, irreverently, as a pictogram on a couple of books he'd written and self-published in his thirties. He was a Stanford grad, but if there's one thing Jeffrey couldn't stomach it's blowhardedness, particularly in academia. In 2014, at the age of fifty-seven, he killed himself and I heard myself sharply scold him, to no one, standing where I was alone absorbing the news: *Goddamn you, Junior.*

He was the oldest and I was the youngest, with nine years between us in the lineup, but I can see from my spontaneous cry that I'd already long ago begun to think of him as a junior, as if we had closed the age gap between us, if not even reversed it. I had already been aware of a kind of surpassing—not the stark physical kind directly in front of us with him dead and me still standing, but in other intangible ways.

Regardless of this—junior or senior, oldest or youngest—it is Jeffrey's suicide that will eventually bring me back to my mother. It won't be immediate or even soon, but ultimately, his sudden, incomprehensible death is what leads me to turn the knob on that decades-closed door at the end of that long corridor. It is what sets me walking along it toward that junction up ahead—my mother making her way in the other direction, unaware—where we will eventually cross paths. One of us clocking out and the other clocking in for her shift, like janitors.

The last time I saw Jeffrey had been just a few years before, at a great summer party at my sister's house, in our hometown, where a few of us had remained. The occasion was the high school graduation of our beloved niece—an outdoor lamb roast celebrating my sister's oldest daughter and her classmates. I drove down from New York and did the cooking for the party, because my sister had a serious and unbudging work conflict on that same day. So in her stead, I'd spent the day hustling in their kitchen to knock down the prep list, while Michael, her husband, corralled my two preschooler boys into "helping" him as he dealt with the lawn and the swimming pool and the firepit and the lambs outside. Just before guests began to arrive, my sister slipped in right under the wire, and, wasting not one second, relieved me so I could run and take a shower while she sped her way through a final kitchen tidy-up. She put all the furniture and the dog bowls and the floor mats up on the counters, then she swept, then she vacuumed after the sweeping. Then she mopped once with liquid soap for the dirt, then got new clean water and did a second mopping with polish—for the shine—then she washed the mop itself. Like a surgeon before surgery, she pumped dish soap into her dish-gloved hands, washed thoroughly up to the cuffs, then tugged off the squeaking gloves and left them to drip-dry by stabbing them onto wooden spoons sticking out of the crock by the stove.

"I just need it done a certain way, Gabs, and I prefer to do it myself," she'd said apologetically, as if she needed explaining, and I'd replied, "Oh, Meliss, please, I totally know, do not even worry. I'm the same." And ran upstairs to shower, shampoo, floss, brush, tweeze, and moisturize.

The sun slanted, and the dusk dropped into all the crevices, as roughly a dozen cars started to pull up the driveway and people arrived out on the lawn. They paused to admire the lambs roasting on their spits over a long, narrow bed of coals; they traipsed in and out of the house, the screen door slamming each time. Soon there were kids cannonballing and jackknifing out at the pool. I saw Jeffrey arrive, take a seat at the firepit, and set a bottle of wine, open, at his ankle. When I was dressed and in a fresh apron, I finally had a minute to go outside to hunt down my own two boyos, to start to think about boiling some plain pasta for their dinner, and I found the maniacal maniacs, looked after by cousins, being pushed to terrifying, thrilling heights on the tire swing. They are eighteen months apart, here on this evening at the tail end of their toddler years, and their modesty has not yet kicked in. They refuse to be clothed; they insist on running around naked. But in the countryside they always ask for shoes; they dislike being barefoot in the unfamiliar grass. I find them otherwise buck naked, screaming fear-joy, with ice cream stains on their faces like clown makeup.

This idyll—what my sister and her husband have done here, all these years, with their own kids and kids' friends, with my kids, with what's expanded through our marriages and contracted after our divorces and separations—reliably, still, at this time, manages to end up as some version of this exact summer evening lawn, with its gathering of friends and family and food and drinks and brightly burning fires. I've had a lot of professional success in New York by this time, but this evening's golden-hour tableau of a sturdy and abundant home life has remained elusive in my personal world. It's what I eternally dream of, what I live for.

I'd had a piece published in *The New Yorker* by then, and as I made my way across the lawn that evening, I found myself flushed at the warmth of being enthusiastically greeted by old hometown friends who generously congratulated me on it. But as I paused by the firepit to say hello to Jeffrey, he seemed physically uncomfortable and standoffish. He found himself, he must admit, stumbling over a detail I'd gotten wrong in the piece. He was sorry to have to mention it, but he was not only disappointed that I'd missed it but also incredulous that the copy editors at *The New Yorker* had missed it. It was in a passage I'd written about something I thought I knew so well: those indelible childhood lamb roasts my parents threw every

summer—like the very one we were creating here this evening—a family tradition, with the animals roasting over coals,
the paper-bag luminaria flickering at stream's edge, the glow-
in-the-dark Frisbees, the long reedy branches of the surrounding weeping willows. I felt I knew every detail in my bones.
But I'd written, and it had made it into final copy, that the
lambs had been skewered onto applewood branches to be set
over the coals, and Jeffrey was now in front of me, agitated,
struggling to contain his frustration.

"It's just not even possible, Gabs. Apple branches grow too
crooked. We only use ash. It has to be ash. Only ash branches
grow straight enough to skewer a lamb onto, not apple. How
could they have missed that?"

He threw up both hands in a gesture of incredulity mixed
with resignation, as if we were soccer players on opposing
teams who had clashed, and the referee has blown the whistle
on him, the wrong player, instead of on me, and there's nothing he can do about this injustice but walk away with his hands
in the air, shaking his head. *The New Yorker* is the ultimate
authority, the midfield ref who has ruled erroneously in my
favor and published my flawed piece—and he was galled by it.

"That's all I'm saying, Gabs. I just don't know how they
can call themselves *The New Yorker* and have missed something so obvious."

I nodded apologetically and agreed. "Oh. Crap. I didn't
know that about the branches. That makes the narrator unreliable, then. Ugh. If the reader spots the writer's mistake, the
writer's then untrustworthy."

"Exaaaaactly!" He groaned his long, bodily relief that I
understood him and that I agreed. "You see?" He quickly

turned to the others around the firepit with whom he must have just been arguing this detail, and gestured in my direction as if to say, *Look! The foul is hers and she admits it!*

But he seemed soothed. His affection for me returned. His body relaxed. In a newly good humor, he continued.

"But, Gabs, you know, no offense. I'm just saying, *The New Yorker* hasn't been what it used to be ever since Tina Brown took over. If they let you publish that, this is the end of American Literature, don't you think?"

The way he included me there—"don't you think?"—with that invitation to agree with him about my own role in bringing about the downfall of American Literature, left me with the unmistakable sensation that I was in some way out-maturing or outgrowing him. I remember noticing in that moment that if he'd likewise had something published, my own response would've been simple and sincere: *Hey, man! Nice hustle!* And I remember grimacing through my disappointment as I corralled my naked maniacs back indoors for buttered pasta and hot baths, knowing that I would need to keep a much greater distance between myself and Jeffrey going forward. But I never imagined it would be the last time I would see him.

WITH MY MOTHER, those thirty years earlier, I had known in my marrow that it would be the last time. Not that it had been explosive or that there had been some volatile episode. In fact, it had been strangely calm.

A routine phone call like so many dozens, maybe dozens of

dozens, we'd had up until then—me on my end in New York trying to describe something about myself or my experience or my opinion on some matter and her on her end in Vermont saying, "Well, no, Gabri. You'll think differently when you mature."

This summary dismissal was commonplace with her and used to send me into fits when I was a kid. As a ten-year-old I would graffiti my bedroom walls in ballpoint pen with outrage—*I hate Mom forever! She is a bitch!*—which she would discover upon entering my room, and meet with an eye roll to the heavens and an "Oh, please, can't you be more imaginative?" But somehow on this particular day, in my early twenties, I was not moved to protest or yell or defile the walls. I was simply realizing in a profoundly serene moment that I had already reached the outermost limits of what she would ever be capable of seeing in me. It stunned me in the way a great discovery can stun—as if a whole new room had appeared in a house I had otherwise been living in my whole life. It didn't occur to me to explode. I just knew with such profound certainty, as one knows very few things, that if I didn't put the phone down and get away from her that very instant, I would perish.

Over the next dozens of years I would take it pretty hard from various of my siblings and family friends who found my decision not wholly incomprehensible but still, somewhat too strident. Jeffrey not the least. "It's harsh, Gabs. That's all I'm saying. Pretty harsh." But, in the moment, I wasn't harsh with her at all.

The certainty was, if anything, exhilarating. And I said goodbye to her in a nearly exuberant state.

"Mom! Unbelievably, this is the end! I am going to hang up the phone now and I will never speak to you again. This is so weird, so unexpected, but this is the very last time I will ever speak to you, so goodbye."

And then I did as I said I would; I put the phone down and walked away.

DADDY-O QUITS SMOKING

M Y FATHER I'D like you to meet at the very beginning, before any of us are lost or dead or cut off.

There will be plenty of time up ahead to retrace the steps, to examine how a whole family is tugged asunder and shipwrecked—each of us like lost silver cutlery and bone china tableware, strewn across the ocean floor. But here now, where this story begins, you should really meet my dad when we all—as a family—are like that great gleaming ship just setting sail on its maiden journey. I'd like you to meet him—The Bone, Papa Boner, Ham, Hambone, James Harvey Peterman Hamilton—in the bright excitement of morning.

Behind his back, we call our dad The Bone, and we find him delightfully, irrepressibly *de-Bone-aire*. He has long sideburns, drives a Mustang, wears aviator sunglasses, signs his name like it's a hieroglyph.

He is not concerned with legibly knitting together a series

of letters in deference to the notary or the clerk or the secretary who files such paperwork. Rather, he slashes out a bold pair of lines and a hovering simple dot: his mark.

I find it dazzling that one could be so disobedient. So non-compliant. I thought you had to meticulously ink out every single letter of your name so that the bureaucracy would not be inconvenienced by your unwieldy and unbridled individuality. But our dad is unapologetic, if not even proud. Daddy-o!

IT'S THE EARLY 1970S, before the divorce, in the family home in Pennsylvania. He comes downstairs into the kitchen and crumples his pack of Camel filterless cigarettes and declares he will never smoke another cigarette again. And he doesn't. From that safe shore of morning, he told of the wild night he had just endured drowning in his own lungs, choking and racking on a smoker's cough so prolonged so bloody so mucosal as to feel cystic and fibrotic. He was so close to dying in his own lung fluid that a mortal terror seized him. Our mother turns from the sink where she is standing and just stares at our dad. Incredulous.

Our house was in many aspects enormous—downstairs a great room with a cathedral ceiling, a dinner table the length of a luxury car, a kitchen with a six-burner restaurant stove—and yet also, in many true ways, miniature. Upstairs where we all slept, like moles in a nest, it was a warren of tiny bedrooms and cramped attic spaces and narrow sharp-cornered left-then-right corridors. You could hear the pigeons cooing in their little pockets in the stone walls as you lay in bed in the mornings, and, at night, the needle crackling the grooves on your sister's record player just above your head in her attic room. And yet still, it felt like it would've spanned a quarter mile from end to end if you could have laid it out straight like a rail, from their master bedroom at one end to the last kid's cubicle at the other.

Our mother had bat ears and spider senses and witch's premonitions so attuned that a child's minor cough from the attic room three hallways away, a nocturnal whimper, or the dream-state moan of a toddler behind a closed door at the end of yet another hallway had her instantly alert, at the bedside— rushing me, or one or another, to the toilet to throw up, to the medicine cabinet for chewable aspirin, to the sink for a cold washcloth. So pricked up were her senses and so light was her slumber that she never missed. She heard you rustle the sheets on the bed long before you rolled out of it onto the floor.

I ended up with this, too. I inherited this high-frequency maternal cochlear sensitivity, this one ear cocked to any shift in the somnatic silence. And even from the leaden bottom depth of midnight sleep, I, too, when I became a mother, could hear one of my own children start to salivate and the curiously rhythmic licking and swallowing from across the king bed, and I was instantly up, rushing to get them a bath towel to vomit into. This, a direct chromosomal DNA gift from my mother: not only a sixth sense, but a hyperactive one.

And now she stares at my father, with his dramatic story and flair for telling it, hurling the crumpled packet into the garbage, his vivid and convinced retelling of how his nightmare night had passed—and she is incredulous. She has her own theatrical tendencies, and she looks at my dad with operatic incomprehension.

"*Pas. Possible,*" she protests, each word its own sentence, and an exercise in French diction. Her grandfather back in Lyon had sent his great baritone across the foggy and thick white sheet of footlights to the topmost tier of seats in the grand opera house there, and her own father knew a stage well for twenty-five years as first chair violist for the Boston Symphony Orchestra. She herself had painted on winged black eyeliner in the lightbulb infinity of many a mirrored dressing room and tied up the satin ribbons of her pointe slippers before she'd glissade out onstage, as one of les corps de ballet at the Metropolitan in New York City before she'd been married and had children, which is just to say: It was long and ancient in her own chromosomal makeup, this flair and tendency toward the theatrical, the dramatic, when she Maria Callas–ed her disbelief up to the last row of the balcony. In our case, the balcony that held the potted plants and ferns and ficus of their open 1970s modern master bedroom suite upstairs. "*Pas. Possible!*" She had not heard a sound all night.

She insists he dreamt it.

I am too young to have been witness to this miraculous morning—which I've been jealous over missing out on for decades—but I've heard the story so many times, I can see it exactly, as if the memory were my own. All of the family gathered there in that kitchen with the pearly white dish soap in the glass bottle on the ledge above the sink: Jeffrey leaning against the cabinets waiting for the toaster to release its catch; Todd and Simon sitting at the round butcher block with their spoons buried in milky homemade granola; the tabby cat sprawled in a patch of sunlight on the terra-cotta floor. And Melissa on the little stone bench near the fireplace, her knees up under her stretched nightgown making elephantine breasts on her foreshortened body, kindling wood crammed into the cubby beneath her ankle-less feet. Our dad recounts the terror of his night, ashen and undone, while tossing his life's last packet of cigarettes into the garbage can, and we sit rapt and riveted. Our postures nearly in rigor at such credibility, and veracity; such a vivid, detailed, true story.

But not her. Not our mother.

She's not having it for a second.

"Not possible, Jim. No, not even possible."

She has utterly no doubt that she would have heard it. And she declares there is not a single possibility that it was anything other than just a dream.

But still, lived or dreamt—and frankly what is the difference to the one who has dreamt it—he never smoked again.

From a pack-a-day man to nonsmoker in the span of one life-altering, amniotic night's dream.

BEAN COUNTERS

AT THE TIME of his quitting smoking, he's got five children under the age of eleven, a wife—our mother—who still affectionately calls him Ploppies, and a theatrical design-and-build studio one town over and across the river in what used to be a mammoth, wooden-domed roller rink. Enormous sets for Broadway shows and industrial expos and even for the Ringling Bros. and Barnum & Bailey circus are built there and then trucked off to Detroit or Corning or New Haven. The guys in the back of the shop who build the sets have sawdust in their pants cuffs. They smell of creosote, machine oil, even faintly of lead from the flat rectangular pencils tucked behind their ears for marking stencil cuts on the sheets of plywood. They are sharp-minded, careful, all of them angle-circumference-torque and muscle guys, dry humor and salacious wit. The clock over the bandsaw bench has a handwritten sign, in all-caps red marker letters, that looks like it was made by someone who never finished the eighth grade and says, THIS CLOCK WILL NEVER BE STOLEN. EVERYBODY IS WATCHING IT. And there's another one in the coffee station, with raised green lettering like an official government parking sign, that says, OSHA IS NOT A CITY IN KANSAS. Reed, who runs this union shop, has two blunt cocktail wieners on his right hand where his fingers used to be.

My dad, himself a lifetime member of two separate unions—stagehands and scenic artists—has his studio up front, where he designs the sets they build. He wears a charcoal-gray suit, a collared white shirt, a tie. He pulls out of the thin, piercing blue light of his drafting printer sheet after curling sheet of gray, damp paper, so wide he uses both hands, like he's one end of a pair of washerwomen readying bed linens for the clothesline. He slides them into Plexiglas tubes reeking of ammoniated developer—so painfully pungent your eyes water even if you are wandering at the faraway end of the hallway, admiring the huge industrial paint sinks and peeking into the men's locker room, cupping your giggles into silence at the calendar of naked women the guys have hung back there.

In the tubes the gray paper sprouts blue veins, and when he spreads the drawings out under the taut strings and the horizontal ruler of his tilted drafting table, you see he has summoned out of nothing an entire detailed world. He conjures out of the warm blue purr of his printer the scrims and proseniums and curtains, the towers and roundabouts and panels that fly, the catwalks and grids and backdrops of what will be in Act One: *The fairgrounds in Minneapolis, Minnesota,* in Act Two: *The ballroom of the Hotel Brevoort, New York.* Even *A square of wood set on a circle of wood* will end up rendered in a veinous anatomic grid of lights, curtains, and flywalls on that gray paper, each mechanicals sheet individually embordered with the logo of his firm: *Design Associates;* the name of the project: *EQUUS,* written in his distinct all-caps handwriting where he refused to put the spines on his E's or the backslashes on his M's. He drew a shaded bar representing an inch. A circle with a plus sign for a PAR can. On that gray paper my dad can even hang moonlight.

HE HAD WANTED to be a painter—studied at Brown then transferred to RISD, then did some work toward a master's degree he never finished at Yale—but came out discouraged and, instead, ran a scenic design-and-build shop for the next thirty years.

"The world doesn't need another mediocre painter," he warned us, his kids, as explanation for his decision to turn away from his dream of painting and devote himself instead to a trade.

On the rare and brief weeks he would join us on the family summer vacations—to Maine, to Corsica, to Bénodet, to the modest shingled cottage on Cape Cod where the chickadees would alight on your cupped hand if you sat statue-still and held the sunflower seeds arm's length from your chest—he unfailingly brought a tin box of watercolors and one of those thick-leaf sketchbooks and painted rather competent dreamy scenes of the harbors and the blousy geraniums hanging in all the blue window boxes.

A private sketchbook once a year on summer vacation— barefoot, in the harmless privacy of your backyard wicker chair? Permissible. Charming even. But any overreaching ambitions ought to be scrupulously shelved so as not to burden the world with what it didn't need. I believe we all took it very seriously, this point of view that one should muster the same self-discipline he had. That we all should refrain from littering the world with any dilettante-ish efforts or minor private achievements likely destined only for the landfill of Mediocrity.

We may have already started to win little elementary school still-life drawing prizes and little classroom poetry contests and more than our share of junior varsity athletic trophies, one of us with a remarkably high score on an IQ test discovered after a troubled meeting with the school guidance counselor regarding his disruptiveness in class, another accepted to Mensa by the time he turned sixteen, but even so, in spite of some of those early encouragements from other quarters— school prizes, teachers' commendations, our essays, our scores, our photo in midair kicking in the winning goal in the local newspaper—giving the five of us early indications to the contrary, he reminded us always of the dullness of mediocrity, of self-indulgence, of the certain peril in imagining oneself as anything other than a Summer Vacation Watercolorist.

He was discerning. To be discerning is to be disciplined, a specialty practiced by specialists in their fields: the jeweler who can examine the diamond and detect the flaws, the art appraiser who knows it's a lesser work of the series by that painter. To be discerning is a way of being expert, exceptional and separate, above, apart, abler, more astute than others. To be discerning is to be my special father, who can reject his own dream of becoming a painter because of his self-diagnosed mediocrity, and turn instead to a thirty-year career of plywood, staple guns, bandsaws, pipe and drape, of design-and-build, industrials and theatricals, rock shows, the rotating booth at the '64 World's Fair where Lee Iacocca introduced the Mustang, even the traveling sets for the Rolling Stones. To be discerning is to deny yourself becoming the painter you wished you could be.

I thought of it as an exceptional and admirable model of self-discipline and scrupulous self-inventory. I had wanted to be a writer my whole young life, but, as an adult, I mustered the same discipline and surrendered myself instead to restaurant and food service: a trade. I considered myself fortunate that I'd been made to understand the value of Standards, and of the pride and worth in meeting them. And if I felt I couldn't meet them, I held that it made me somehow mature and precocious and flinty that I'd been shown at such a young age how to discern, how to self-select out.

"And, look, Gabs, nobody wants to be an also-ran."

He was home on a weekend, in dusty jeans and a striped button-down, laying a corner of a masonry wall that would eventually anchor a wooden deck he was adding onto the house. I was old enough to read and went around clutching a cherished book from which I could not be separated, sleeping or waking. I carried it with me at all times, but even so, I managed to bring him each next heavy stone from the pile that he beckoned to with his trowel, as he set in place the one before it, while gripping my book with the other free hand.

I didn't know what it was, an "also-ran."

"The other guy on the ballot; the one who didn't win. Who is ever going to remember Barry Goldwater?" he asked, as demonstration, and of course I couldn't say; I was six years old.

"Exactly."

With a protective mien, he confided his instructions.

"Don't ever advertise it unless you've won it, Gabbies. Don't ever put on your résumé that you were a runner-up. That you were short-listed. It's like bragging that you couldn't win."

IN HIS EVENTUAL CAREER, he did not seem hindered by the possibility of his own mediocrity. And he remained candid in assessing his own talents as well as others'. He openly advocated the *borrowing* of good ideas as long as you knew who you were "quoting," and he thrived, pursuing his work as an active pleasure, rather than as a tragic concession. It never held him back once he cut it loose, this sense of his own mediocrity as a painter. In design-and-build for the theater, he delighted in and seemed liberated by the recognition that having new or unique ideas was not required. I felt the same way when I gave up on the pursuit of writing and turned full-bore toward restaurant work. A kind of liberation borne of dispassion for the fallback plan. A sense of shrugging resignation, as if to say, *Well, I only need to be good enough for this pursuit, and I can clear that low bar. So, let's go!* And he seemed further freed by the relatively relaxed standards that set-building called for, as I also did when I understood the minor proficiency that restaurant cheffing required: mostly just cleanliness and consistency. Henri Matisse said that the work of the artist is "illuminating the fog that surrounds us." Which is much more daunting than roasting a nicely seasoned chicken and making sure to scrub down the pan afterward.

I suspect our father was impatient with the exactitude and the persistence required to penetrate that fog, the unrelenting dedication that is required of great art, and even of great craftsmanship; master carpentry scaled precisely to one-sixteenth of an inch, but in his looser world of "it's good enough for theater," where the plywood sets just had to make it to Cincinnati and then would be struck and dumpstered, you scaled to *roughly the inch.* Artists had to make sense of the human condition and architects had to complete rigorous math and engineering studies, but designers could set up shop without so much as a diploma and hang out their shingle and simply shove a desk in the corner for a credentialed draftsman to deal with the nuts and bolts.

"Everybody else does the bones and makes sure the thing doesn't fall down," he loved to say of his work. "I do the romance!"

He eventually designed everything with this freedom and was prolific: houses, restaurants, additions to old houses, strip malls, public parks, shopping plazas, summer stock theater. He recited poetry with the same inexactitude, sometimes paraphrasing and eliding phrases that didn't suit him. He threw epic dinner parties using recipes torn from magazines, which he transferred in his own handwriting into his cooking notebooks, dutifully citing his sources, yet giving the impression of his having authored them. He learned to slalom race and mogul bash but pursued the more theatrical ballet skiing, with its looping helicopters and 360s, until he got good enough at it that it caught your eye if you were going up in the chair. He told long double-punch-line jokes and short zingy one-liners; picked up vivid and ribald and moving anecdotes wherever he heard them and made them his own later; he became a true raconteur even of adventures and tales and poignancies not his own, but which he could deliver to magnificent effect at all the ceremonies requiring toasts, all the last-call nightcaps, all the dinner parties, all the weddings and funerals and holiday gatherings of a man's lifetime. He was already good at it when he told us of his harrowing night's hell coughing up his own wet lungs and only got better at it with the years. "Nobody has any new ideas," he'd say, again and again and again, "it's all just in knowing who to steal from."

SO REMARKABLE WAS his way of knowing who to steal from and what to do with the material he stole that, once in his possession, it would be tailored and made better by his taking it. Pablo Casals, Pablo Neruda, or Paul the Apostle—or probably none of the above—may have been the one who originally said, "She was my student until she became my master," but when our father stands up at my sister's wedding and tinkles his glass with the silver fork and lays that one on the room, it is only Daddy-o we have seared into our hearts, as we raise a glass of champagne and smile through wet eyes at his pure romantic heart beating in front of us. We are not thinking of proper citation, rightful ownership, or dutiful ascription.

To him, you did not need to be famous, nor a master of your craft, to be useful and borrowable. Anything tasty, wonderful, odd, scandalous, harrowing, charming, funny, dirty, or eccentric would be considered. Tragic was fine. Heroic, also good. Cantankerous, lousy, criminal, or chaste; underdog, top dog, sly fox, paper moon, cool cat, or country mouse alike, he would recognize what there was to use. And he would leave

behind the dead weight of any precise factual debris, any unwieldy mitigating truths or details if they proved too cumber-
some to allow liftoff.

He was quick to discern which parts of you and your experiences might likely be squandered if left in your unfit custody.

For those of us who "borrow"—I inherited a streak of this,
too, in my own genetic disposition—it can be justified as an
act of thrift or conservation; a genuine worried disbelief that
one might waste that which we find so precious, like when a
dinner companion has left half of her portion still on the plate
for the waiter to clear: *You're not going to let that go to waste,
are you?*

Some stories can be so pitifully sad, or damning, or com-
promising that they are left untold, because the tellers fear
they themselves will be found pitiful, and pitiable, or culpable,
or vengeful and petty, grotesque and obscene, by even telling
such stories.

You have to have the necessary appetite for telling them, in
the first place. And be willing to gain the weight it will require
to carry them.

Me, I always ask first—"Oh, man, that is a good one, can
I please steal that? Do you mind if I take that?" I am too self-
conscious, too concerned with others' feelings to just freely
ransack their material. But he'd reach right over and nab it
with his fork, your uneaten story, even if you were still chewing. And I thrilled at his delightfully frank bravado around
this propulsion to "borrow" other people's lives. I was titil-
lated by his utter unapologeticness about what he lifted in
broad daylight with a scallywag's wave to the security camera,
as if the greatest talent of all was to know the difference and

to rob the right house. As Mr. Pablo Casals actually did say, "Let us not forget that the greatest composers were also the greatest thieves. They stole from everyone and everywhere."

I was sometimes proud and flattered when he stole my experiences and made them his, even while I often blanched, stomach twitching, seated at the dinner party table, Daddy-o recounting wildly embellished and revisionist accounts to the crowded room, even when he took such egregious liberties with the "text" of my experience, even when he assigned me feelings I wasn't feeling and intentions I didn't intend. It can be nauseating to be publicly mischaracterized by someone and even more distressing if that someone is not especially talented. But he was mightily talented, and it was something pretty exhilarating when you were young to have ranked in your dad's eyes as plagiarizable. *It's all in knowing who to steal from,* and he was stealing from me!

I was utterly taken with his remarkable showmanship. His knack for placing the poignant detail, allowing silent beats, burying the lede, using what he would call a "by the way": "Oh, and by the way . . . she'd been picked up by the cops that afternoon!"

You squirmed in your seat at his dinner parties, twelve years old, sixteen years old, nineteen years old, twenty-four years old, thirty-one years old, forty-two years old, outwardly giggling at the Total Rewrite, receiving their winks and side glances at what a sassy monkey you are—*What a handful!*—while his dinner table or barstool audiences looked back at him, eyes glittery. "Good night, Jim. Good to see you! Take care!" And they shake his hand and head out into the night. You're so proud to be his punch line that you collect all the crumpled napkins, empty the ashtrays, giving yourself a moment to walk off the sting of having been so egregiously mis-characterized, like a midfielder shaking off a ground ball to the shin, and then, you get right back into the game. Without even realizing it you start to go out of your way to drum up a life of new sassy episodes that will feed him a supply of fresh raw material. And you begin to see yourself through his eyes, as a plywood panel of the scenery in his story, a stage prop, a character. And this becomes a lifetime's lifestyle.

Whenever I find myself in a story I can't bear, I become a second-person remote *you*, a body's length removed from an *I*, observing. No longer the me, here, my actual self, I, standing right in the very room, going to fucking pieces.

BUT STILL, EVEN with all of that DNA coursing through my veins, and all of the uncanny ways he is me and I am him, I grow up to be not nearly as brazen as my own father. I am obsessive about verifying and annotating and footnoting. Citing the sources. Announcing whose byline of what article whose exquisite phrases I may retell at dinner parties of my own. Which poet and which poem, declared. Wincing if I spell a name wrong; shame if I mispronounce it. For him, of no concern at all.

In his mind, you and your slavish fidelity to truth and citation: actually a mark of your own smallness, your own pettiness and inability to think big or to see broadly. "But wait, Dad, that's not at all how it really happened," you have sometimes protested, after everyone has left. "That's not the truth."

"Oh, that's for the bean counters!" he dismissed, making a pantomime of a squinting company accountant, mock-pushing up his pince-nez and dutifully penciling in an exact amount on the ledger of his open palm.

That kind of earnest accounting, to be so conscientious in detailing how it really happened or didn't really happen, was it a Tuesday or a Friday, an inch and three-eighths or one and five-eighths, that ledger so fastidiously and meticulously kept of the Truth in one column and the Fibs in the other, he derided and dismissed as the petty concern of the dull.

"Accuracy is for clerks!" he delighted in repeating.

Though he himself never wrote more than personal correspondence, black ink, felt-penned letters and notes, quite possibly he was the greatest writing teacher I have ever had.

FREEZE TAG

WHEN I WAS little I felt the same gushing admiration for Jeffrey as I did for our father, and for a week or two I had a crush on him and planned to marry him. This was before I knew that you couldn't marry your family, when you are so young that all that you know is that you *heart heart heart* that perfect boy so *much much much*. I discussed it with my best friend, Renee, who lived just up the road, and she said she had the same feelings about a long-haired older cousin of hers. We hunted for woolly bear caterpillars, braided and chewed on onion grass, choreographed gymnastics routines on the lawn, practiced the delicate art of making saliva bubbles. *Are you allowed to marry your own cousin? Your own brother?* we wondered.

Her property had portions of meadow and steep hill banks that lined the stream, and our property had portions of meadow and steep hill banks that lined the stream, equally.

But at her house, there were crumbling walled gardens with stone paths, a long keyhole driveway missing most of its white gravel, and a proper name on an iron sign at the entrance— SPRINGDALE. Jeffrey had been allowed to commandeer an outbuilding on the property—a tilting, lopsided potting shed—and he repurposed it into a little fort, which we wandered around outside of, trying to spy into it without getting caught.

There was no routine for whose woods we wandered, whose trees we climbed, whose section of creek we waded in, but it was often her property where everybody from the neighborhood wound up for adrenaline-pumping games of flashlight tag and bombardment and capture the flag.

Or, as on one particular day, freeze tag. A summer hurricane had just days before passed through, leaving hard green-gray skies, pissing little brief squalls as warm as tub water, and swelling the creek beyond its banks. Some power lines had been downed by fallen branches, which brought all the neighborhood kids outside to look over the damage. On this charged and atmospheric day, late in the afternoon, a game of freeze tag has erupted. All around us a swarm of neighborhood kids have gathered and are tearing through the wet grass, knees buckling down the steep slope of the hill to the stream, getting tangled in the giant weeping willow at stream's edge.

Caught up in the excitement, we dash out from behind a stand of tall paintbrush spruces and start running madly in the direction of home base, willy-nilly joining their game in progress. I see Jeffrey locked in place midway down the hill to my left. These boys are all about cunning and strategy, speed, stealth, subterfuge, and surveillance; all I know how to do is run around in circles in delirious terror of getting caught while giggle-shrieking. But somehow, out there in the wide open, there is Jeffrey, frozen on the hill, beckoning to me.

Impossibly, he's been tagged!

He whisper-shouts to me to come and rescue him.

I scream to Renee to go on ahead to home base without me, then veer downhill to free him. I am too little and too giddy to have any cunning, or to be any captain's glad pick, but I know what it is to be on a team: You decoy within view of the prison guard, you set distraction fires, you taunt the "it" team, you create a diversion so that your mate can release your captured brethren from their prison on the big sawed-off tree trunk where they huddle, you elbow-crawl as silently as you can through the grass behind the guard's back. You rescue your mates.

Here, now, I find myself with the extraordinary mission and responsibility of liberating my oldest brother. He is the one uniquely allowed an eleven P.M. bedtime. And I'm just the little one with lemon Jell-O for brains and tooth fairy money fresh in my pillowcase, but he has somehow gotten himself frozen in place and by some miracle I haven't; I have the power to free him. As I approach, he doesn't reach his arm out to me, as you would in a relay race baton pass, so we can run off together. Instead he remains a planted statue with his arms close to his body as I near and he says, "Tag me, Gabs, tag me here. Just a little closer. I'm frozen like this." I leap the one remaining stride left between us and land one foot dead center in the squishy, soft brown poo of Renee's golden retrievers, shocking cold, waterlogged dog shit squishing between my toes. Jeffrey explodes, howling, cut in half laughing maniacally, nearly spastic with the hilarity as he rights himself and runs off, back in play. I remain planted in the poop, unable to move, staring down at my foot.

One of the dogs runs over and starts licking her own poo off my foot; I can't believe what I'm seeing. I have the natural impulse to swat her away. And yet it's also helping so much. She's getting almost all of it; it will then just be a matter of dragging my foot through the wet grass to get to the stream, stepping into the churning cloudy water and twisting a little in the gravelly bottom, digging my toes in; then it will all be gone. I can get back into the game. I had no idea that there were dogs who ate their own shit.

At last, foot washed clean in the whorling stream, I walk, panting, back up the hill to the group, where they're counting out teams again to start another round. Jeffrey is coming down now from the peak of his hysteria, self-possessed again, but seeing me approach, he re-erupts into spasms, his car-starter laugh breaking his face open.

It's contagious; I join him with my own giggling.

"Oh man, Gabs, that was a good one, right?" He opens his hands skyward with a kind of apologetic, *I'm sorry but the opportunity was just too good to pass up. I couldn't help it* shrug. And it's easy to agree; it *was* a good one. Clever, harmless, precise. Astute. His knack for predicting my behavior and response. The perfection of his timing—while teammates zigged and zagged all around us on the hill and leapt in and out of bushes in a mad dash for home base, he could still calmly carve out the brief mental space required to pull off this little bonus thrill. Rigging up a clever prank within a game—all without getting tagged by the enemy team in the process of coolly setting it up. The strategic positioning of his own body in spatial relation to the poop. The faking of his own captivity. The perfectly calculated number of steps he had figured I would have to take to get to him.

I was in awe of how clever he was, with the way he stood coolly, patiently waiting. He adored the international soccer star Pelé, and how Pelé played what they called "the beautiful game," and Jeffrey played the beautiful game wherever he was, whatever he was doing. He had control, finesse, joy, and timing.

One day in high school, Jeffrey's physics teacher brings the whole class to the gym and gives them each the same sheet of paper with the challenge to see who could get theirs the farthest, from one end of the gym to the other. Immediately they all start folding and creasing, while Jeffrey coolly waits them all out, doing nothing with his sheet of paper. Only after they have all sent their paper airplanes miserably nosediving and veering then crashing short of the half-court mark, Jeffrey stands up, crumples his sheet of paper into a ball, and sends it hurtling the entire length of the gymnasium; it goes sailing overhead, crashes against the far wall, and, with energy, force, and velocity to spare, bounces back inbounds.

But he never lost his taste for the less elegant tomfoolery. The gags that hinged on the gullibility of others. Once, on a family ski trip, he got up early at the lodge and replaced all the salt in the salt shakers with milk before everyone came down for breakfast. At a family graduation luncheon, he poured a splash of ice water on the vacated chair of a cousin who had gotten up to use the restroom, and when she retook her seat, Jeffrey exploded in laughter as her face registered the startling sensation. He was always inviting Renee and me to punch him in the stomach as hard as we could while he held us at arm's length by the forehead and we punched the air, still thinking it could be done while he knew it couldn't. Maniacal hyena laughter. And king-of-the-jungle roar.

Even with my own bare foot booby-trapped in dog shit I was in awe, giggling right over the little blue tears forming at the corners of my eyes from how meanly, yet exquisitely, it smarted to be duped by the one you loved so. Admired so.

I imagine his suicide, when I learn of it, as glorious and clever, specific, aesthetically organized, well-timed, and even humorous. I imagine his tree painstakingly selected. It's already darkly funny, as soon as I hear the news; there would be no mistaking ash for apple in this case. He'd been a professional woodsman and cut firewood for a living. I was sure he'd picked a good tree. I imagine him going out into the woods wearing something rugged and canvas. Blue and French. His wide-brimmed hat. His turquoise ring. I imagine a noose of worn leather. A ladder of hand-hewn wood with pegged rungs. Given the lifetime of good-natured pranks, I even imagine puckishness and hilarity as he jumps. I picture patient timing, as the sun finally crests the dense foliage and sends its high-noon "Okay, now!" beams. I imagine his explosive laugh as he drops from the branch, two arms thrown up in loose, apologetic victory, his eyes glassy with laughter as they always became when so wildly self-entertained. I imagine the great neon canopy of a magnificent yellow oak overhead, shivering from the vibration.

ROADKILL

Growing up feels to me, at every stage, like a "coming to"—like I'm a person who has blacked out during a lively party in full swing and groggily starts to gain consciousness, putting the images and faces in front of her into coherent order—in a slow and inchoate progression, not only at seven but at thirty and also at forty-three and so on, a lifelong progression of understanding the order of things I hadn't understood before. But in early childhood, the incoherence that becomes especially whole and round involves the six other people all living with me in the house: This is a family, these are my own people, I have parents and brothers and a sister and they have personalities, individual characteristics, hobbies, desires, comings and goings, uniquenesses, identifying qualities, eccentricities.

And together we have rituals, systems, congruent cohering events that make us who we are as one. We have an annual lamb roast. And we stud tangerines with whole cloves at Christmas. And we go to Cape Cod to visit our grandparents, where we play miniature golf and dip steamer "piss" clams into broth, then drawn butter, and on the way home we are allowed to sit in the back of the Volvo station wagon with the hatch door up and our legs dangling down, the sandy road ribboning out underneath our bare feet. We burn the wine cork with a match at Halloween and rub our faces with the blackened ends to look like soot-covered, train-hopping hobos as we wrap up potatoes into kerchief sacks and hang them at the ends of sticks to complete our costumes. We giddily make up words—*Boneificent, Bone-a-fide, Bone Vivant*—and create a whole vocabulary centered on the family nickname: Bone. We are a first-person pronoun, a single word that perfectly holds all seven of us inside it.

And one day there is a white-tailed deer hanging from a tree branch out back in our meadow, still warm, bleeding out. And it belongs to Jeffrey, who has hauled it home from the side of the road, where it had been hit and killed by a car. Its eyes are rimmed black, and its eyelashes are long and bristly, but the body is thin and underfed and unattractive. Still, the eerie power and presence of a whole animal hanging from a tree in your yard is considerable.

Who drags home a roadkill deer? My spectacular, fascinating oldest brother is who. In my mossy terrarium of a child's mind he has dragged it in his arms 140 miles for all I know because a mile is a yard is a year, because things that are heavy are as heavy as boulders. Things that are far away are as far away as galaxies. Why he has done this, what it is doing here in our meadow, I cannot even imagine; for me it is just to admire and to behold when I wake up from naptime and wander barefooted out back to the meadow one afternoon.

He'd long ago set up his little anthropologist's fort in that abandoned potting shed at Springdale and had been collecting the debris of natural life and spontaneous death from the woods and fields we were surrounded by. There were rows and rows of tiny teeth and the small skulls of possums and coons in that potting shed. He'd already amassed a collection of arrowheads, which he'd learned to hunt for as a twelve-year-old, while kicking around on wet mornings in the plowed fields along the Delaware River where our hometown nestled, when the chances of finding them were made best by the previous night's rain. He fantasized already, at twelve, about the day he might live as a hunter-gatherer, as the earliest peoples had lived twelve thousand years before; a way of living he romanticized: to be one with Nature.

The shelves of his shed were lined all the way around with antique glass bottles that he found in the woods where he wandered, greened from the insides with algal mildew. There were heavy blue glass and white ceramic insulators fallen from the telephone poles and power lines. He had arrowheads, incomplete skeletons of roadkill squirrels and turkey vultures, and, stabbed into jars like flower bouquets, he had eagle, owl, hawk, and pheasant feathers. There was animal fur, stone, quartz, shale, flint, and moss. All sorted and pleasantly arranged. There were five clay bowls he had made in his high school anthropology class—as early preparation for what would be his senior class project, in which he proposed to make prehistoric tools and then to live in the woods by his own wits using them to survive for the week.

This quite handsome boy, his chin-length hair tucked behind his ear, in an off-white dashiki and cutoff painter's pants, is looking for something, already as a teenager he is seeking a way to live that synchronizes with the natural world.

It's the 1970s, with Earth, Wind & Fire, the Isley Brothers, the Rolling Stones, and the Beatles bleeding out of the stereo speakers in his room, and this boy wants to "live off the land." His school is all about creativity and independent thinking, and the final projects one must complete for the year's end are to be designed by the teenagers themselves. When he could have been home in his little alcove room at the top of the steep narrow stairs choosing to more or less comfortably write a senior research paper, Jeffrey walked himself out into the woods about two miles from our home, to practice living close to the land for the week of spring break.

To—in the vernacular of his time—*get back to Mother Earth*.

In his backpack—assembled with great concern and indecision about what to include and what to leave out—he carried books, paper, pencils, gourds, gloves for flint working, a sleeping bag, pants, bow, arrows, a jacket, sandals, herbal teas, a knife, a toothbrush, a canvas bag, salt, nylon cord, a metal pot, a sheet of plastic, matches, and sprouts. I had to read over that again a few times when I later found it in his collected diaries—he packed *sprouts*.

As our mother would eventually teach us all to do, Jeffrey could identify wild asparagus and milkweed and watercress, fiddlehead ferns and nettle, and for the week of his project, he expected to use this knowledge to collect and live on what he found in the woods. For protein he planned to hunt pheasant

and groundhog, but his hunting and trapping skills were yet so
unpracticed that he ended up devouring the only things he
managed to catch: three raw robin's eggs and the nightcrawler-
sized liver of a two-foot-long snake he killed with his knife.

To me, with our nine years' difference, he is like a mesmerizing postcard of a very attractive foreign place that I feel
strong passionate wishes to know more about, to someday
visit, as soon as possible. When? When can I have a shed? And
tools? And walk into the woods for days alone? And wear a
dashiki? And be so amusing that I laugh myself to tears?

THE ROADKILL DEER is not in the journals, but I am certain
I remember it from around this time. It is not a figment of my
child's imagination: eyes wide open, rimmed jet black, long-
lashed and hanging from a tree branch in our back meadow to
bleed out, 130 pounds of roadkill.

After it had bled out he harvested the hide and the teeth
and the bones and even the tendons; he stretched the sinew
and the silver skin from the muscles into long crude threads,
which, after sun-drying, he used to sew the seams of the pants
he had fashioned from the hide. He had started, and made
significant progress with, the waistband and the thighs when
he realized that the hide from one deer would not be enough
to make a full-length pair of pants, so there would be other
deer, more roadkill carcasses to redeem and recycle. This did
not happen quickly or sequentially—it took years and several
more hides before he would finish them. He taught himself to
tan the leather, but the results were uneven, so the pantlegs

ended up darker from the knees down. He also ran out of patience for making the threads by sun-drying the sinew, so he finished by using brass rivets as staples the rest of the way.

But still. Those pale, smoked-butter deerskin pants sewn together with deer sinew and fastened with brass rivets always brought you to a full appreciative halt when you saw him wearing them. When you understood what they had started out as—a warm lovely creature wounded and left on the road, then a strange corpse, hanging upside down by the hind legs from a tree branch, and then, with such persistence and attentive ministration, the attractive, soft, useful object that they had become.

GILGAMESH

WHEN HE WAS nineteen years old, Jeffrey let the screened door of the kitchen close behind him, stepped off the gravel of our front driveway onto the paved road, and hitchhiked to Africa.

Leg by leg, highway to interstate to ocean to continent— with his thumb out, he made it through our downtown with its cozy bars and its clutch of shops and then he crossed the narrow bridge over the Delaware River into New Jersey, where Main Street dead-ended three traffic lights later at Villa Vita, a whitewashed cinderblock pizza shop, then took a left at the intersection onto the four-lane highway that led him fifty-five miles later to the freight pens, marshaling yards, container lots, grain silos, gravel domes, trucking depots, and oil tanker berths that make up the greatest hub of transatlantic travel on the Eastern Seaboard: Port Newark, New Jersey.

Here he got himself onto one of those ships that defy

imagination. Ships that require teams of men working round the clock, forklifting and rigging on and off the crane beds, that take a thousand man-hours working in continuous shifts to move the merchandise, the thousands of containers of propane, glitter, sand, coal, shampoo, motor oil, yogurt, lawn fertilizer, and on this day, with his backpack so fastidiously packed with his Dr. Bronner's 18-in-1 natural soap, his foil-wrapped quinine tablets, his prescription bottles of anti-malarial chloroquine and Lomotil for diarrhea, his tissue-paper journals, and his archival ink pens—like one more piece of cargo—young Jeffrey was also taken out to sea.

ON THE DAY he hefted his backpack in the kitchen and readied to leave, I stood stiffly by the unlit fireplace and smiled saucer eyes, beaming enthusiastic adrenal smiles but caught off guard and blinking back a sudden tearful surge of emotion. I had not known. I was seized with the terrible understanding, only at this moment, that our crew, our unit, our team—my family, the one I only recently woke up to—was not going to stay and belong to one another for a lifetime but, instead, anybody around me could just up and go when they felt so moved. I was only aware of things that mattered to me, the tangibles, the many-colored stripes on my favorite T-shirt, the profound and uncanny stare of the glass eyes of my stuffed raccoon, the splintered roughhewn one-by-fours of my bedroom ceiling that I would gaze up at while daydreaming on the carpeted floor. But in that fifteen minutes I understood that a family was leavable.

I'm about to turn ten—I have long known the route to

school, the stops the bus makes, my home phone number, and I can perceive the lewdness of jokes or the seriousness of discussions around me even if I don't understand all the technicalities of them—yet I am still completely oblivious to how things work: Will he go outside and put out his thumb and find a ride to Africa? My child mind stumbles at the imagined land's end, the place we've been shown on the huge pull-down classroom map where one bright-yellow continent sits suspended in a turquoise-blue ocean far away from another fire-engine-red one in the distance. Can you just put out your thumb at the edge of the yellow one and a boat will pull over? *Hey, son, where you headed? Zaire? Hey, me too! Hop in!* And yet, even in adulthood, decades later, I still short out at the water's edge and find myself incredulous. I realize that this story about him has been told the same way since that day and has never been expanded or en-nuanced and I have inherited it wholesale, without questioning it: Nineteen-year-old Jeffrey Hamilton simply walked out our kitchen door and hitchhiked to Africa, they say! We say. I say.

I ALREADY HAVE some mental picture by then of what it is like to travel by ship because I'd already been on one. The summer when I was five and Jeffrey was about to be fourteen we went as a whole family to see my mother's family in France, and we went there on an ocean liner, the SS *France*—at that time the largest passenger ship in the world.

We were expected to pack our own suitcases, so I fastidiously rolled all my cotton undershirts into bundles, tucked the bundles in under the hard case's satin lining, and fastened the elastic belt that held everything in place, then triple-checked the metal latches once closed. I practiced lifting and setting down the suitcase in my room. I practiced carrying the packed suitcase down the hall and down the three steps at the end of the hall and then back up the three steps and back to my room. I could lift it and carry it, I was now sure. On travel day I wore my favorite dress, a high-collared starchy black poplin, with a white fleur-de-lis pattern in rows from neck to hem like on a blackjack machine when you pull the lever, my ears already pierced with tiny gold hoops. We got on the train in Trenton that took us to New York, where we would catch the boat.

I minded my own suitcase, nursing the whole while a deadly fear of being separated from it. At the curb in New York, we realized our family was too numerous for one taxi, and we would have to split up to get to the pier. And we had to hustle, to divvy ourselves up crudely, bags and people hastily splintered off into different cabs, amid a tremendous urgency, trilling with police whistles and shouts. The whole while I was rigid with anxious uncertainty, not knowing whether my suitcase was in the trunk of my cab or my dad's cab or was now, mistakenly, in the trunk of a taxi that had sped away with some other family to some other place. But then we did arrive at the immense pier, and miraculously there we all were, spilling out of cabs, reunited, our luggage in a formidable stack on the asphalt, our group made whole again, a blob of mercury scattered into droplets but now satisfactorily drawn back to itself; I found myself ebullient with relief.

I had been terror-stricken by the casual disappearance of everyone I had ever known. Jeffrey, Todd, Melissa, Simon, Dad, everyone speeding off so carelessly and cavalierly, with no one looking back out the rear window to make sure we were in caravan. When we pulled up to the pier and I saw we were reunited safely, I started shouting to my mother, "Look! There's Dad! And Jeff! And my suitcase! Look!" Such thundering relief in my five-year-old chest, pounding like applause for the disappear-reappear magic trick of it all.

My dad finished paying the taxi drivers, and we gathered our suitcases and started moving toward the ship. We faced, as far as you could see up into the sky, the chalky black expanse of the ship's hull, a colossal black steel letter V, held in its watery slot by thick braids of rope. To me the ropes resembled a giant lumberjack's boot laces, and what I understood was that we would have to now climb up those ropes single file, to get on board. I fell silent with the realization that, with no time to practice or rehearse, now on the spot I had to strategize how I would hold my suitcase in one hand and shimmy up the ropes like we'd learned in gym class, but without everyone looking up my dress and seeing my underwear, and without losing my grip and plunging into the water below.

We made our easy way along a wide, gently sloping carpeted walkway, but I felt crushed under the weight of my worry, in mental preparation for the physical feat just ahead, even as we gracefully and gradually zigged, turned right at a landing, and then zagged, all of us ambling up along this carpeted gangway that deposited us into a lounge like at an airport.

And then I saw it: We were already somehow on the ship. I started shouting, "We're on the ship! We're all already on the ship! I thought we had to climb the ropes!"

And my whole family erupted in laughter—and even though they were laughing at me, at what I hadn't understood, I was thrilled to be able to join them, to be able to see now what they saw, to know what they knew, to laugh at what I hadn't seen before. It felt exhilarating to have gotten here, to be fully five years old and at last in on the joke, to have finally caught up to everyone, as if now I was part of the We and we were at last a one. And everything to me felt new and fresh and indestructible and permanent—lag bolts welded into forever place. It seemed to me that we ourselves were at the exciting beginning of our own voyage—not this immediate practical one directly in front of us, on our way to France to visit my mother's side of the family, but this other long jolly and enduring experience of Familyhood that would span on and on and on to some unseeable horizon.

AND THEN JEFFREY was gone.

When he made his way to Africa, he did it with the engine of neither academia nor church behind him—he was not a funded researcher and not a missionary; he was a nineteen-year-old kid keeping a diary, looking for some mythical and idyllic unsullied world, some way of life that took only what was needed from the earth, and did no harm in the taking. Naïve to his own imperialistic ideas, undaunted by his own ignorance, blithe to the implications, and swept up in the ethos of his hippie era, he made his way to the center of the Ituri Forest in what was then called the Belgian Congo, and he lived and worked and slept and hunted with a tribe of Mbuti Pygmies. He bought a small hut and later installed a windowpane at great expense so he could write his notes at night and keep working even when it rained. He danced, drank, and haggled with Kisangani villagers, and sometimes, when no missionaries were near to disapprove of him, he wore nothing but clear plastic sandals and a loincloth made from pounded inner tree bark.

I was electrified by the pride of being his sister. What a thing to be able to say about myself on the first day of elementary school social studies class, when we were introduced to cuneiform and the first story ever written: As far as I was concerned, Jeffrey was our very own Gilgamesh and he entered his own cedar forest in search of the path to a long and untroubled life. "My brother is in Africa living with the Pygmies!" I blurted. That I didn't understand the difference between Africa and ancient Mesopotamia was unimportant— for the bean counters—I would boast of his being two continents away, of his drinking manioc wine from gourds, of his dodging Gaboon vipers in the forest and battling fungal rot between his thighs, of the way he would slice open the ringworm sores on his body with an X-Acto knife and then sprinkle a dusting of yellow powder from a capsule to treat them, as if he were seasoning a steak. I recounted how he went along on an elephant hunt, the excitement building as they came upon huge depressions in the mud "the size of dinner plates: elephant tracks!" and shared his marvel at the finesse and effortlessness and elation with which they felled a fourteen-thousand-pound mass. Four strategic lead Pygmies running from behind to get in under the magnificent creature, one Pygmy per leg, and each in unison stabbing their spear into the back of each knee, then dashing away as the beast collapsed. Later, they got it onto its back, tented open the belly, and built a bonfire inside, to cook the meat. He wrote home of these events in neat, fastidious penmanship on long blue folded airmail tissue-paper letters covered in stamps that arrived months after he'd written them. And I told these stories of his at school and loved what they—his stories—made of me, and who I became in the telling of them. I was made interesting by his interestingness.

I KNOW NOW that what may have been sparked by the kicking up of a few arrowheads on damp mornings as a twelve-year-old boy had become a gaining pursuit as he got older. There had been a sixteen-year-old summer digging eight hours a day in the caves at Pech de l'Azé and following that, a course taken at Virginia Commonwealth University in experimental or "living" archaeology. And in his senior year of high school, just before that tromp out into the woods near our house, he had gotten himself a meeting with the British cultural anthropologist Colin Turnbull, who impressed Jeffrey so much.

What is the difference between nature and self? Jeff found himself asking. The profundity of this coming from a teen-aged boy caused our orbit of surrounding adults to raise impressed eyebrows at Jeff's precocity.

And then there it was, a spring day in 1976, his tourist visa finally approved and furnished, making possible the central event of Jeffrey's lifetime: his journey to the heart of the Ituri Forest. He wrote home eight-, twelve-, sixteen-page letters, and in them revealed not the excitement you would expect, but moreso his disillusionment and perhaps also the early seeds of something off-kilter, something askew, something to attend to. I saw only the fantastically tellable stories about gross-out meals of termites fried in oil, and the elephant on its back, with the hunters climbing up onto it "like ants on an apple core," as he described it. But it's there. An obsessive streak, a fixation with what vexed him, and he was easily vexed, always in conflict with one or another villager or the chief, often bored, even more often angry, but I was too young to pick up on it. I couldn't believe he had eaten termites! And they tasted "exactly like french fries," he said. There was also, I only see now, reading back over those letters, such a dull and blunt-headed vestigial boyhood still clinging to his bones as his soul-searching careened between the profound and the ridiculous: *What is the difference between water and a beverage?* he wrote. A rather concerning departure from his earlier *What is the difference between nature and self?* If I'd been an adult, one of his parents, I might have noticed. And worried.

"I feel so depressed!" he raged.

But the only things I could see were the things that mattered to me: that my amazing brother was in Africa, living in a hut.

NO

WHILE JEFFREY WAS away in Africa, our mom announced her wish for a divorce, and without any warm-up or rehearsal or preview, suddenly our dad was not living at home. We were all called in to the formal dining room on a weekend afternoon. Simon and I sat silently on the floor vying unsuccessfully for the cat's attention by pattering our fingers on the oriental rug and our mom said, "Jim, it's over and the kids and I think you should leave." I have never been more blindsided by a piece of news, before or since, and never been more incensed, before or since, to find myself conscripted in favor of a move I was desperately not in favor of. But in the moment, my fifteen-year-old sister suddenly cracked open and started crying hard at the table and I remember thinking, *Jesus, Melissa's really acting soft. And so immature!* And so I continued lying still on the rug, as if indifferent to the news, stomach down, fucking around with the cat. My dad cleared his throat, and cleared his throat, and cleared his throat, but I can't recall if he ever said anything. He moved out to a kind of gentlemen's rooming house a few blocks away from his work called the Swan Hotel, an old creaking building with a bar downstairs and private rooms above, rentable by the month or the week, with shared bathrooms at the end of each hallway.

He came back to the house one night late when I was the last one up doing dishes and cleaning the kitchen, and he stood outside, haloed under the yellow porch light. He tapped at the kitchen door. I saw him through the heavy glass and hurried to let him in but he remained at the threshold, swiping his feet on the mat, shoulders hunched, collar on his big navy winter coat up around his ears and hands jammed into his pockets.

"I need a blanket, Gabbies. There's no heat at the Swan. The pipes froze." His face was hollowed out. His eyes, dull and watery.

I sprinted up the stairs on all fours, silent as a cat. Tiptoeing down the pitch-black hallway to the giant wicker chest where blankets were kept; this was at the very foot of yet another set of narrow stairs that led up to where my mother, having vacated their master bedroom, now slept in what had been Jeffrey's alcove room. She was already asleep; the door was shut at the top of the stairs, no light coming through any of the cracks. I lifted the lid of the chest as slowly and incrementally as I could—a burglar stealthily lifting the kitchen window sash while the unwitting family sleeps upstairs. But the wicker lid and the brass hinges squealed shrilly into the silence in spite of my caution. In the summer our winter clothes lived in this chest, and in the winter our summer clothes lived in it. She was so organized and orderly. A family of seven, fed, dressed, ironed, and pressed, and on a budget. A household well-ordered. Clothes folded, sorted, and put away by the seasons. Older kids' clothes altered and mended to fit the younger kids. Hand-me-downs saved and saved and saved from the first child to the last. Twice a year she took us to see June the seamstress and had her measure us with her yellow tape, clutching straight pins in her teeth as she hemmed or took in or let out. Extra bedding or table linens my mother ironed and stored here, perfectly good but not needed bedspreads, all then kept in here, this massive wicker chest with squeaky brass hinges.

She hears the creak, and she calls down through the dark, stopping night in its tracks, and me at the bottom of the stairs in the hallway, holding the lid midair. "What are you doing?" I freeze in place.

The seconds are ticking. I hiss up the stairs, in a throated whisper, "Dad's downstairs and needs a blanket. There's no heat at the Swan and he has pneumonia." A few extra coats of saturating pigment I hope will make an adequate impression.

And without switching on her lamp, she calls down, "No."

Letting it penetrate, this No, I let down the lid on the wicker chest and creep away down the hall. But I pause when I get to the head of the stairs down to the kitchen and my waiting father.

Unable to descend with my terrible message.

Briefly—a bright spark in my brain—I detour to my own room, a quick right and then a quick left, in the center of the warren, and stand at my own bed with its one blanket and its one sheet. It's cold inside, too, even with working heat—she keeps the house low on the Honeywell dial, to save money and to conserve energy. But it's not the cold winter night that makes me hesitate and draw back from grabbing my own blanket to give him—my dilemma is childish, the dilemma of a ten-year-old: I love my blanket. It was the most cherished item I owned, with its jet-black fake fur and its brown velour trim. It didn't quite cover the top of my twin bed, it did not even drape down over the edges of the mattress, but if I laid still and slept in a ball, it covered me well enough, and I refused any other. In our house there was no thumb sucking, no "binkys," baby foods, plastic toys, pacifiers, sugary breakfast cereal, footed pajamas, or choreless lazy Sunday-morning cartoons. It was all Nakashima coffee tables, Steuben glass, and homemade granola. This black fake-fur number with the brown velour trim was as close to a filthy pastel security blanket as you would ever find in our parents' spectacular castle of art, design, and aesthetic devotion, and I couldn't part with it.

I go back downstairs to the kitchen and turn my father down.

"Mom says no."

And I watch him stagger away.

SOON AFTER JEFFREY killed himself, I became aware of a circulating bit of hometown gossip that claimed he had called our mother, in a pinch, to ask if he could come and stay with her in Vermont for a bit and that she had said no. And then, a few days later, he was found dead, had hanged himself. At fifty-seven years old, he was decades past the hour when an anguished son might reach out for his own mother and yet the rumor claimed he had.

Someone had forwarded to me an email exchange in which two gossiping friends from our hometown—strangers to me—share back and forth between them the shocking news of Jeffrey's suicide, the morning after it occurred.

Hola amigo, I wanted to know if you'd heard that last night Jeffrey Hamilton committed suicide?

Heyyy you still practicing your Spanish? I heard he wasn't in good shape, apparently.

The saddest part is he announced last week he was leaving the area altogether since he'd lost his business over the winter, including his truck, and was going to live with his mother . . . until she said "No, don't come, I don't want to see you." And I thought I was a bad mother!

I flinched when I read that, in part from an impulse to defend my own mother, but in truth, mostly startled with a terrible recognition. I sat back in my chair and sighed heavily to the empty dining room where I'd been working, papers and computer spread out at the dinner table. *Oh, Jeffrey. Oh, you poor fucking puppy. She said no?*

There had always been a lot of "No" with her. Routine and mundane No:

you'd like to eat one of the hard-boiled eggs in her fridge
you would like to stay up one hour past bedtime to finish
    your book
come inside from the sleeting cold and stop being healthy
    outdoors
bring a friend home
go to a friend's house
wear pants not skirts

join Little League
quit ballet
have a sweet in the afternoon
sleep in on a weekend morning
watch a program on television
be a vegetarian
feel crushed that you lost to the Astros
talk on the telephone with your best friend about
    toothpaste and shampoo
keep your cherished stuffed raccoon
decide for yourself which of your possessions you have or
    haven't outgrown
wear your hair long
wear your hair short
have red gel toothpaste not baking soda powdered
    toothpaste
use Farrah Fawcett shampoo not Herbal Essence pine tree
    shampoo

With her there were daily dozens of the regular garden-variety Mom No.

But she could hit some thornier Nos in there, too, not quite as mundane.

You miss the school bus in the fifth grade and your school is 4.8 miles away; in the fifth grade you are ten years old but it's already long ago understood to be a *don't even bother asking* No, so you don't even consider turning back to the house to get a ride. Instead, you walk the gravelly edges of the long country roads that pass along cornfields and deep woods and distant housing developments. An aggressive dog runs out from a yard set back from the road, lunges at you, and, with bared teeth, takes a chunk out of your thigh. You run-walk-run-walk-run-walk the rest of the way blubbering and panting, fire in your lungs, and then in the classroom, six rows back, your stiff, brave face is betrayed by the blood now trickling below the hemline of your pleated skirt, and your teacher, Miss Tuthill, spots the blood and is suddenly coming toward you with urgent concern. She walks you to the office, where they call your mother, and you wait for her to come and pick you up and take you for four stitches and a tetanus shot at the medical center in town.

Divorce settled, house appraised, contents divided after negotiating the terms, a young, enterprising Jeffrey is hired to drive her rightful half of the household to Vermont in his truck. He drives at a conscientious and loaded-down fifty miles per hour for eight hours north. He's twenty-one, twenty-two years old, freshly home from his African excursion; she's already been up there settling in, with Simon and me in tow, for almost a full year. He rolls up in his big blue truck, stretches after the taxing drive, paces the yard to shake it off; she comes quickly out through the screen door, drying her hands on her apron, cooing with her affectionate *l'il precious kitten* voice that she uses with all of us no matter how grown we've grown. "There you are, Jeffrey, poor baby, such a long trip." She crosses the yard, arms up, not to embrace him but to be embraced, as if she is the fussy little baby and he is meant to be the soothing adult. He leans in stiffly for this customary greeting, where she makes little mewing baby-love noises while you are expected to be kissing her on both cheeks in the French custom, but she wants real fleshy kisses, not glancing pecks. He disentangles himself and steps up onto the porch, makes his way into the house—it's a modest old farmhouse on a remote dirt road she's renting until she gets her money from the divorce and finds a place to buy. He washes his hands, then paces around in the kitchen, goes to open her fridge—a cold chicken leg, maybe a cold beer—but from across the room she slaps her hands sharply on her aproned thighs, halting him. "Ah, No!" she barks. It's always been an especially sharp No in her house to ever just help yourself to something to eat.

ON ITS OWN No is just a dull household object, a butter knife of a weapon; a simple No could not harm a child, could not cause a man to stagger, could not be responsible for the suicide death of a grown man. It would be outrageous to suggest that our mother said No to Jeffrey and that then, as a consequence, days later, he killed himself. But this person in the email seems to be saying exactly that. *And I thought I was a bad mother!* The quality of our mother's mothering is obviously mine and only mine to decide. But still. I can't get the question out of my mind: She said No?

She had once been so keenly spectacular in so many ways. The chewable aspirins. The ears hyperattuned to the nocturnal whimperings of her stomach flu babies. Prescient. Supernatural. When her babies were babies. At your bedside before you even called for her, as if by premonition.

But she has little facility and a very short fuse for the later parts up ahead. The roughhousing and mayhem and pranking and thunder and squabbling and disobedience, the record players and electric guitars and indoor Frisbee tosses and forgot-to-unplug soldering irons of the five evolving humans upstairs, no longer swaddled in their baby clothes, no longer little blind kittens in their shoebox mewling tenderly for an eyedropper of warm milk. By the time we are five children under the age of fifteen forcefully rubbing up against her ankles like demanding cats, some now with cracking adult voices, with emerging willfulness about subjects more profound than eating one's vegetables or submitting to one's bedtime, and with distinct individual volition of their own, she cannot tolerate it. She says, openly, frankly, in a French-tinged diction, as she hockey-pucks our family cat across the kitchen floor with a forceful swipe of her ankle, "Ah la la la la la la, I fucking hate cats." We drive her into sudden rages. And she allows herself to unleash on us with a wooden spoon, until she is spent.

We find this funny.

We make jokes about it to our friends at school: "You could smell the ratatouille!" we howled, laughing. Snatched in haste from the counter next to the stove and the simmering Le Creuset pot of whatever she was cooking, the first implement she could put her hands on as she came thundering up the stairs to tamp down whatever unruly business we were brewing up there—was this the day one of us decided to jump from the bedroom balcony down to the TV room couch holding an open umbrella à la Mary Poppins? Or was it the day she discovered that someone had found and helped themselves to the little foil packets of dark chocolate she kept hidden for herself in the utility drawer? We recounted these wooden spoon episodes to our schoolmates in Technicolor detail, seeking both to impress them and also to benchmark our own experience against theirs. *Is this what everybody means by "got a spanking"?* we wondered. It's not that her rages were administered tepidly or symbolically or like a convincing yet toothless performance of the theater craft of stage combat where the person being beaten slaps the stage floor with their upstage hidden palm while the audience sees the villain standing downstage land fake blows on the inert bodies of the child actors playing children.

Not at all; they were real. They stung like hell.

And they often smelled of onion or anchovy or garlic. In the midst of a shellacking you would smell the unmistakable fragrance of piperade, or veal stew.

But they were not The Thing; I don't believe they are what made it possible for Jeffrey to step out back in the middle of the night, rope over his shoulder, in search of a tree. I will eventually have a chance to run this by Simon, just to double-check that I'm not downplaying it, and he nods vigorously in agreement: This is not what hurt. Yes, shocking at first, yes, terrorizing on your first inaugural experience, but soon even you could see that the woman was simply agitated out of her right mind in those brief minutes. You could be taken down by one of her episodes in the afternoon but as soon as that very evening, you'd be back in the kitchen with her as she prepared dinner, you sitting on the long cushioned bench under the yellow curlicue telephone and poring over the giant Sears Roebuck catalog while she chops onions and gets the oven going. She gets two glasses from the cabinet and pours you a chilled bitter lemon and herself a chilled gin and bitter lemon and you share a cocktail hour together while she cooks dinner. She hums. Whistles. Smacks her lips in exaggerated satisfaction at what she is stirring at the stove—slurping from the cupped end of the same wooden spoon she has earlier grabbed to run upstairs with—and finding it delicious, crows, "Nummers!"

Remember that time when she broke the first spoon and

had to run downstairs to get another? Jeffrey rocking back in his chair, spitting saliva from laughing so hard. This is great physical comedy, complete with pratfalls. *She had to come back with an even bigger spoon. And she broke that one, too!* You can see where this is headed; the punch line writes itself. Soon she is grabbing a stray three-foot length of molding, left over from some one or another of my dad's ongoing house projects, and chasing Jeffrey up the stairs.

On a decades-later visit to Vermont to introduce his fiancée to her future mother-in-law, Simon brings as a gag gift one of those enormous wooden spoons that hang over the menu boxes outside of tourist restaurants in Europe, and they take mirthful photographs in the sunny front yard, arms around each other, with my mom holding the spoon and mock-threatening the camera with it. We find this hilarious.

Even now I find those rages, at least, logical. I would go so far as to say reasonable. Not in their magnitude, their unbridled force, nor sometimes their eye-popping volatility—I'll never be able to find enough narrative height to look down and coolly argue the reasonableness of a grown 140-pound human beating the living lights out of a squealing 60-pound child with a greasy wooden object. There's one episode I will never forget, when I had dared to complain to her yet again about being forced to wear an annoying wool skirt and its matching scratchy sweater. But it was certainly comprehensible, retrospectively, in the way of things that matter most to me. I mean: reasonable in their emotional explicitness and coherency. I have never and will never do well with the unspoken yet intimated, the unsaid but broadcasted, the elided, the implied, the signals without the accompanying instructions, the unarticulated yet palpable emotional curriculum of another human being. It is not those clear and explicit baton-wielding crackdowns of hers against the disorderly conduct of our try- ing to become our sovereign young adult selves that come to mind when I am pawing and sniffing the dirt for answers to Jeffrey's suicide. When I am considering and evaluating the quality of our mother's mothering, it's this No I find trou- bling. And then all the other butter knife Nos of her lifetime that I find myself starting to track, like a bloodhound, my tail wagging, baying up at the trees with a frenzy to alert my han- dler to the strong scent I am picking up.

The No to giving you a lift to school if you missed the bus, the No from behind the closed alcove door at the top of the dark stairs that bade you to take the weapon of her message and stab your father with it, the summary No to the opinions you express and the feelings you describe, the No at the end of the phone call where you have lost your business over the win- ter, and your truck, and were hoping to go and stay with your mother "until she said No." That No.

EVERY SUICIDE CARRIES with it—to some extent—an ac- cusation. And for those of us remaining, it is ours to confront. What portion of this is mine to answer for? Who can say how suicide works? I would never lay that at our mother's feet. But once on the scent of No, unleashed by this hometown gossipy rumor, I can only wonder if they might have been lethal. Not directly lethal like a gunshot to the brain, but a meandering lethal, like a criminal negligence. I have spent quite a bit of time wondering about all of that No in aggregate, and if it can act like some kind of accruing red viral load that has finally accreted to such a blood level that on the day you decide to kill yourself, if you happen to pause on your way out to the tree with your ladder and think, *Should I call my mother for some help here?* you already know the answer will be No and so you just get on with it. For months that stretch into years I will wonder if this rumor is true. And I will worry, if it does turn out to be true, if I will be kind enough, if I will find enough kindness in myself to consider both his anguish and, my god, hers, too. Will I be kind or unkind? Either way, I realize I am going to have to fact-check, to finally call and speak directly with my mother. To step out into that long corridor and start walking toward the answer.

Part Two

JIMINY CRICKETS

WHEN OUR PARENTS split up, most of the kids were accounted for in natural, chronological fashion— almost everyone was on their way to something: on their way to Africa, on their way to college, on their way to a semester abroad. My brother Simon and I, still just a few years too young to be on our way to anything, would've preferred to stay put in our hometown and in our family home, but it was agreed that our dad—so often away for work—would not be up to the job of looking after a seventh- and a ninth-grader, so we were taken with our mother, mid-semester, to Vermont. The local school she enrolled us in was one long hallway, with as many kids in all of the grades combined as we were used to having in just one class. And all of our subjects were taught conversation-style, around conference tables, as if we were heads of companies at a meeting with other executives. We made films and recited poetry and we met David Dellinger and

Claes Oldenburg and we sheared sheep and staged a reading of *Of Mice and Men*, and there was a girl with lesbian moms, and a girl in a whole-body brace for scoliosis, and a handsome boy who knew how to calve dairy cows, another who bow-hunted, and almost everybody smoked Salem menthol cigarettes out in the parking lot after class. After parting with our new lively friends, the long walk home across snowy open fields was fresh and invigorating, but to cross the threshold of her house and latch the door behind us was to be swallowed.

Her temporary furnished rental suffocated me; our beds were not our beds, the sounds of the house were not our sounds, the smells not our smells. The lamp I read by was made of beaded white milk glass in the shape of a mushroom cap, which somehow made me feel belittled, and every time I switched it off before going to sleep I thought, *Why the fuuuuuck am I here?* I don't know what my brother was thinking, across the hall in his own suffocating room, but decades later, when I am going through my mother's house and cleaning up her boxes and boxes and boxes of saved papers, I discover that he may have been pissed off, too. The headmaster at our progressive Vermont school made it clear that Simon would not be welcomed back the following fall. His final evaluation, handwritten: "I feel your attitude toward the school was condescending and arrogant . . . You played us like you play soccer: toy with the opponent, find a weak spot, and score." I feel defensive on Simon's behalf reading this, even so many decades after the fact, and I protest out loud, alone in the sunroom where I sit with her papers. "Hey! We were going through some shit, man! Lay off the boy!"

At the end of this school year, as soon as school let out in

June, she released us back to our dad, in spite of his incompetence. And we did not need persuading.

I will NOT live with you again, my mother and I declared to each other.

I was standing in front of the sink in that kitchen on Ha'penny Road, waiting for Jeff to pull up in his truck to take us back home, but who said it first and who said it in reply? We both emphatically said it, and while the feelings were reciprocated, I still considered it a smug victory that she'd said it first. I felt like it was an accomplishment, a point of adolescent pride that I couldn't wait to share with Renee, when we—after a whole agonizing school year spent cleaved from each other—again sat cross-legged in the grass, reunited at last. With a shrugging, feigned indifference, I bragged how my mother had sent me packing, feeling that it made me somehow tough, and interesting.

"And she was like, I never want to live with you again. And I was like, well, I never want to live with you again, either." We dragged on our cigarettes stolen from her father's soft pack of Carlton 100s and practiced blowing smoke rings on the exhale.

When Jeffrey returned from Africa, he found he had returned, as he wrote in his journal, *no longer a boy, but a man.* He would find that while he was away not only had he changed, but so had we. Even the house itself had changed; there were strewings of my dad's old married life and stirrings of his new divorced one in every half-empty room of the warren. He'd moved back in after she left and reclaimed the master bedroom, but the little alcove room at the top of the stairs where my mom had decamped during the separation remained empty; there were dead wasps in the sloped sills of the skylight windows.

A reek of mildew in the washing machine.

Stale nuts and rancid oils in the pantry.

Moths and shaggy webbing in the flour.

Oxidized vermouth the color of copper in the liquor cabinet.

Our dad did not know how to run a household that contained perishables.

Jeffrey had been tasked with driving up to Vermont with his truck, with depositing into her garage some last stray furnishings and items that she had finally been granted custody of following their divorce: the two minor Picasso line drawings that had hung in the plant room, the windup clock, the twin beds, the elaborate medicine chest that resembled a Victorian dollhouse with porches and windows and double doors where she used to stash perfume bottles and hairpins and lipstick tubes. And he was asked to bring us back home on the return trip, once the truck was emptied. Simon rode up front in the cab, and I rode in the back tucked in with all our stuff, much of it packed in garbage bags, which crackled furiously the whole way, whipped by the wind all the way home. Through slanting sunlight in Massachusetts, through dusk in Connecticut, and through the glittery fantasia of red taillights and the platinum and gold headlights of interstate nightfall we drove south—until we at last reached our home in Pennsylvania.

I wore a maroon cotton roll-neck sweater from L.L.Bean and a bandanna, pirate style, over my braided pigtails, a white cotton drawstring tiered skirt, and Converse high-tops—my thrift-store adolescence in full bloom. And when we reached the outskirts of our hometown—twenty degrees warmer than where we'd just been that morning—I peeled off my heavy sweater, tilted my head back, let my shoulders go finally slack. I banged on the cab of the truck and yelled, "Jeff, take a spin through town first! Just give us one cruise up and down before we head to the house!" A busy green mist of moths and mosquitos and gnats and pollen swirled like a cosmos in the gassy light of the streetlamps as we passed beneath them, rolling down Main Street. My eyes stung from the unrelenting hours of interstate in the open back of a pickup. From this insect stardust, from emotion.

OUR DAD WASN'T home when we got there. He was installing a show in New York City. He may have slipped in a few nights later, for a fresh suit and a change of undershirt, to put a few things in the fridge, but it was kids chaperoning kids those first few weeks. And Simon, like a full balloon whose skinny rubber neck has been pinched between parental fingers its whole life and then suddenly released, zoomed careening out the door in a great cartoon swoosh, propelled by the rushing exhaust of his helium to friends, to parties, to keggers organized in cornfields or at somebody's horse farm. And he stayed out all night, stayed wherever he was staying for days at a time. He came home for laundry pit stops and showers on occasion. Our dad was having some trouble with money. Creditors called in the mornings, and I answered the phone, telling the truth: "I'm sorry, he is not home and I don't know where he is or when he'll be back."

Design-and-build for theater was not going well. What did he "lose" in the divorce, and had he been put in the hole by it?

I don't know. Did he have to pay alimony? I assume so. But how I swooned to finally be back in my room, my room, my room. I am a Scorpio child, and the droll wisdom most circulated among parents of this era was "Never send your Scorpio child to her room as punishment—she loves it there!" It's one of those pop psychology truths that happens to hit the bull's-eye for me. Incomprehensibly, it was smaller now, the door-knob lower, the ceiling much closer; in just a year I'd shot up. Someone had left behind a transistor radio; I lay down on that floor, my feet resting on the black trash bag of my belongings, and mooned with dreamy relief up at the rough splintery planks of my ceiling.

I find a pop station. It comes in clear. After 350 miles in the back of a truck and such a relentless battering by the wind it will take hours for the vibrating tremble to seep out of my bones. I lie on my back on that floor, like a car put up on blocks over an oil pan to drip and drip and drip. "I would've walked head-on into the deep end of a river . . . Someone saved my life tonight," the singer sings passionately. It's tinny, a cheap transistor radio, but the feelings pour like a syrup into the room and become my own. "Coming in the morning with a truck to take me home." Pop song after pop song fills my tiny room, my brain, my chest, a repeated building whisper spills out of the pinhole-perforated speaker and rolls across the floor like low-hanging fog. "So if I call you, don't make a fuss . . . Big boys don't cry. Big boys don't cry. Big boys don't cry."

In some aspects, no different now on the cusp of entering eighth grade than I was in kindergarten, I am still a girl who can lie for hours on the floor of her own room, lost in her imagination, but who is now preoccupied by the Top 40 radio

station, and by her own reflection in the bathroom mirror, in
the questions of her own self-obsessed mind. Would black eyeliner bring out the blue of my eyes? Should I black-henna my
hair? The first week returned to my home I lie there all day
until evening, all evening until morning, lost in picturing who
to become, reveling in the new feeling of having no leash, of
being unloosed in a house that itself is unloosed. I've been
wandering the hallways and roaming around in the unlocked
rooms at the summits of the steep and narrow staircases of
this strangely changed but familiar house. What once held all
seven of us, so snug and squirreled away in our warren—with
the pigeons warbling in the stone walls and the classical music
on the stereo playing all day while our mother whistled along
downstairs, always cooking something in the kitchen—now is
a strange and hollowed-out version of itself. But at the same
time the place feels ripe, possible, open to the adolescent
imagination. A barn floor right after the reaping.

Finally, one evening, it is past dusk, and in spite of how
mature, how jaded, how practiced a smoker I'm becoming, I
realize we don't have anything to eat and that I don't know
what to do to get more food. I've bloomed in some ways but
still haven't in some of the other, most important ways, and
am still unaware of how things actually work. I still don't understand the mechanics, the plain physical details of myself,
let alone anyone else. What does everybody do all day? How
do they come and go, according to what demands and forces?
Why is the house always empty when I wake up and when I put
myself to sleep? Where is everyone? Does Jeffrey have an
apartment of his own? Is his old room used now only for storage? What will I do once that last inch of Herbal Essence
shampoo in the bottle on the tub ledge is gone, how will I

wash my hair then? The freezer is empty but for a box of lima beans, a package of chicken, both covered in frost crystals. And yet only now, this one late afternoon, the sun is slanting, only now that the tremble in my own body has drained, I'm starting to wonder how I will eat, and if I know what the right mushrooms are in the woods if it should come to that, if I have to find my own food. Do I put the brick of freezer-burned chicken directly into the oven?

I call my dad's shop; the secretary-slash-bookkeeper answers, weary and aggrieved, says he's expected back from the city but she hasn't seen him yet, and she'll tell him I called.

"There isn't any food here, just let him know." She exhales her cigarette smoke, the clack of her IBM Selectric never stops while we speak, and says she'll give him the message.

And then, finally, he is home. He arrives late, a brief overnight before he will have to return to the show, the last push before the show opens, clean socks and a few clean shirts and in the morning he'll have to drive back out of town, back to the city, but he's home now. Daddy-o! I come downstairs as soon as I hear him in the kitchen; it's been a whole school year away from him and what I know as home. He is looking worn, hollow in the face, but he has paper grocery bags, and he keeps his gaze in them as he unpacks them on the counter.

"Hey, Dad."

"Heeeeyy," he says, but he is wan and reserved when usually he is bright and delighted.

"Everything okay?" I ask.

"Jiminy Crickets, you kids are so expensive! It's one of those days when I could've pulled the wheel and driven myself right off the bridge, you know?"

He leads with this morbid humor, but there are dark gray

stones where his bright Paul Newman eyes should be. I smile in response to his candor and at the electric charge of being thought of as mature enough to be let in on the dark jokes, the figures of speech—*drive yourself right off the bridge!*—but simultaneously I quickly comb back over the day for what I should have done differently, what I could have done to cost less money. Immediately I start strategizing how to go forward: Could I be a mother's helper? A lifeguard? Could I mow lawns? Clean houses?

Thirteen isn't little anymore and anyway I can't wait to be done being thirteen; my dad always introduces me in new settings with a wide grin, saying, "She's eleven going on seventeen!" and I always swell with pride; it is my favorite compliment and remains so for the next several years. "Guess how old I am!" I command, at any opportunity, any gathering where I am not already given away.

And when they say, "I don't know—nineteen? Twenty-four? Twenty-one?" I levitate with satisfaction.

I can fry an egg but there have to be eggs in the fridge to fry. Suddenly, I see that I cost so much money that it can change the color of my dad's eyes from Hello My Darling Daughter blue to Because of You I'd Like to Kill Myself charcoal. Immediately I understand that I have a rent-free room in which to lie down on the floor and listen to pop songs on the radio but the things that go with living—food and shampoo—I will need to figure out. And quickly. Over my dead thirteen-year-old body will anybody be driving their truck off the bridge because of how expensive I am.

He is gone when I wake up in the morning, back into the city for the next several days. He has left his Walkman cassette player and headphones on top of the bureau in his dressing room: I pop the foam pads over my ears, walk barefoot around the house, push open the screened kitchen door, stand in the powerful sunshine scream-singing along with the Bee Gees: "Don't throw it all away, our love, our love. Don't throw it all away, our love." I kick around in the gravel, sit on the railroad-tie steps, inhale the heavy humid chlorophyll air; down in the driveway I see he has left his car and decided instead to take the bus because it's cheaper than driving.

That afternoon I walk into town and go into the first restaurant I find and ask for a job. I don't know what position to ask for, but I say, "Waitress?" with a question mark and they make me, instead, a dishwasher. I take to the dish pit almost preternaturally. I use the rubber scraper on the plates, then the gooseneck sprayer hose to rinse; I pop the glassware into the checkerboard racks tilted overhead, push the racks into the machine, and pull down the stainless steel arm to make the cycle start—it's a perfect starter job for me, and on breaks I can stand out back by the dumpsters and practice my smoke rings to be ready for eighth grade the coming fall.

THE CAR

I HAVE FALLEN IN love with the Walkman; music just pours into your head—like warmed honey—and makes a soundtrack to your own life, while you are living it. I have a job. A paycheck! A free meal each shift and all the soda I want; I just have to wait until the bartender is free to be able to politely ask him to pull that soda gun from its sticky holster and refill my big glass. The soda is free! The thick haze of deep summer drapes over each day and cushions the nights; there is no curfew. The trees are greener, the breezes breezier, the languidness more languid with these headphones piping their sonic dope into my brain; I walk out back in the meadow, I walk the country roads, I walk the train tracks that lead into town. With lovelorn quivering duets sung by Barry and Andy Gibb pumping into my ears, the meadow is more meadowy, the country is more country-ey, the train tracks more train-track-ey.

The house has an entirely different feel now and it fascinates me to wander around in it, now that there is no one standing guard, nobody there to make you dry and put away the dishes or clean the lint filter in the washing machine, nobody to say *stay out of my room,* to say *keep your hands off my shit!* Nobody is there to patrol the refrigerator, or all of those formerly off-limits closets, wicker chests, china cabinets, liquor cupboards, utility drawers, strange dark corners of the cellar with their old skis and sleds and paint cans and stacked wooden crates of empty bottles. Now my mornings are spent in my wake-up haze, idly wandering the post-divorce house. Every room, every cabinet, dresser, closet, drawer, crawl space, and cubby now can be pulled open and rifled through and examined, like I've come upon some kind of archaeological dig site, and I must examine the pottery shards for clues about the civilization who had been up until recently living here. Nothing is as it was and still hasn't become what it will.

My dad—my dad who can't boil water—is evidently becoming a bit of a chef. My mom is the one who had us eat paella and bisteeya and choucroute and stroganoff—her cooking had been well-known and admired in a wide circle—but it's already been a couple of years now that he has had to endure without her, and he's grown frustrated at having eaten so well in the past and so poorly ever since. He's taken a cooking class—in Paris. He has freed himself from his former helplessness in the kitchen, and he now has his own rudimentary skills, as well as a few formidable tricks; he makes butter rosettes and choux paste swans filled with Chantilly cream. He is fermenting his own root beer and bottling it himself. He has replaced the little round butcher block table where we used to have weeknight family meals with a handsome eight-foot trestle-style kitchen work island. It has a copper vegetable sink dropped in at one end, and at the other end he keeps laid out at the ready, on display on his wide wooden cutting board, his two beautiful chef's knives. Antique Chicago Cutlery knives with carbon steel blades and brass rivets in their wooden handles. I am rummaging around in the kitchen drawers one lazy morning, for matches, loose change, fresh batteries for the Walkman—and there, under the new French waffle weave dish towels he has come to love, I discover the car key. The key to the car that now sits in our very driveway where he left it when he disappeared back to the city for work. A most exciting artifact, slipped immediately into my pocket.

I START DRIVING at night because I don't want to be seen in daylight, constantly stalling out in the middle of the road, unable to figure out the clutch, and I am afraid of getting caught. But then I get better at it—left foot depressing the clutch, right foot relinquishing the gas while shifting—and I start to take some chances driving in the day, too. I can't yet get into first gear without stalling out, but, usually, I can get the car to go by starting in second gear. I'm gambling with trouble, but if I go out into the countryside, *What are the chances I will be seen?* I reason, and soon I start driving at all hours, careful to pull back into the driveway exactly in the position the car had been when I found it. It's rural where we live, and wealthy. People's driveways are long, their hundred-year-old farmhouses sit back from the winding roads, their horses graze in fifteen-acre pastures. I just don't think I'll be found out. Also, the windows are tinted. My newly divorced dad has gotten rid of the family wagon, the old blue Volvo we called the Bone Chariot, and is now driving a green Volkswagen Scirocco with black-tinted windows. Me, too; I've just gotten divorced myself in a way—"I never want to live with you again!"—and now I'm also driving a green Volkswagen Scirocco with black-tinted windows. "Guess how old I am!" I command anybody I meet. I'm thirteen.

SIMON FINDS IT peculiar that the car is not in the driveway where our dad left it.

I breeze into the house one day not expecting to find him there—his teenage intoxication with this new, lavish, unchaperoned freedom is as acute as my own, but his looks different than mine: He has dozens of friends, parties to go to, weed to smoke, keg parties to hit up. I'm still practicing my inhale on a cigarette. Renee's father is going through his own divorce, for the second time, and she has been shipped to her mom's in Massachusetts until further notice. I help myself to the strange, oxidized contents of the liquor cabinet. I walk downtown and sit for hours on the church steps where the juniors and seniors and a few of the dropouts hang out; I smoke pot if they offer it to me and play it cool. I sail into the kitchen, letting the screen door slam behind me, high in my own way, on the newness of everything, on the agency I now have over my time, my body, and on the previously unfathomable mileage I can now travel away from home on my own, way beyond what I've ever accomplished on my Schwinn three-speed or by all that walking.

Not that I have any imagination for the freedom; all I do is try and take myself in the car to the places my mom used to go that I think I can remember the routes to by heart. The farm where we used to get raw milk, the dog breeder kennel we used to pass on the way, the elementary school I have only recently graduated from, the soft-serve ice cream place, the Hansens' house.

Here is another family like ours. In our town there are a notable few—large families with lots of kids, lots of school prizes, lots of photos in the local gazette. We are some of us schoolmates but not all—between elementary, middle, junior, and senior high school some kids, even in the same family, get put in public and some in private schools. But we know one another. Some of the Hansen kids are older by eight months or younger by ten but we are all in the same range, close enough to know that I am your classmate's little sister, two grades be-hind, or you are the brother in that family who is just one grade ahead of one of my brothers in school, and, *Oh cool, your parents are away, too? A couple of friends are here with you for the summer, too? Max is home from college, he's the one in charge? Cool, cool, I'm here, too, hanging out this sum-mer, yeah, we're done with Vermont. Donzo. I just thought I'd stop by. To say hey. Car's out front!*

When Simon confronts me that afternoon as I am passing through, I'm thrilled to confide in him my discovery, to pull open the slim utility drawer by the stove and say, "Yeah, look! I found the key in this drawer!" I tell him this with collegial, conspiratorial, crewmate excitement: *Look, Sime! Look what I found! Look what I got!* I am eager to show him my windfall. He himself is underage and unlicensed, like me, but instantly, incomprehensibly, he becomes my opponent rather than my colleague. He unilaterally decides he is more entitled to the car parked in the driveway than me, his little sister who is already well on her way to burning out its clutch. With a galling authority, he takes the key right out of the drawer where I'd so carefully replaced it and, shortly thereafter, leaves with the car. My Car. What could have been Our Car. I was ready to share the gain. But he now has made it His Car. And there evaporates as capriciously as it had appeared: My Freedom. My adult selfhood.

Whenever I sit in that car,

With the window rolled down and my elbow hanging casually out,

With my cigarette in the ashtray and the radio on,

When I pull into the parking lot at the school I will attend in the coming fall and pop open the sleek metallic green door and step out of the car, one freshly shaved leg making its careful appearance in cutoff jean short-shorts,

I Am All That I Want to Someday Be.

And Simon has just walked off with the key to it.

I am enraged at the injustice of it. The car belongs to neither of us, the car is forbidden to both of us, but I'm the one who found it, and according to my metric: *finders keepers!* He is taller, bigger, older, a little unknown and unknowable, keeps a lot of secrets, secret stashes, secret shortcuts, secret comings and goings I will never know to where or with whom, but also, weirdly, we have never been friends. I've been close with every other sibling at different times—even Jeffrey enjoyed having a little gullible sister during freeze tag and Todd used to pay me a few dollars to rub his calves and feet when he got home from his after-school job sometimes. My sister and I, the outnumbered girls, even with five years between us, have still had T-shirts to swap and earrings to borrow. But there has been no bond with Simon. We've never quite gelled. And here we are on our own in the house together. Every man for himself. I don't see the car for days.

IN OUR PARTICULAR familial patois he is called Sly and the Family Bone, or sometimes a French-accented Simone, or simply: Sime. He can leave with fifty cents in the morning and come back with fifty dollars in the afternoon, not necessarily legitimately. He's rascally, daring, restless; while the rest of us learned to ski by traversing the mountain in elegant swoops, planting each pole for the turns, he would hop off the lift, *shush* to the ledge, then tuck his poles up under his armpits and bomb straight down the mountain. My dad bought him a helmet early on—the rest of us in wool hats, Simon in a white motorcycle helmet and yellow goggles. He gets into hot water all over town but gets himself right out because, as one of the grown-ups says, *He can charm the rats off a cheesecake.* The shopkeepers and the mayor and the police chief and the guy who owns the ice cream shop with thirty-two exotic flavors— they all know Sime and when they stand out on the sidewalk in the morning in front of their shops on Main Street, saying good morning and letting down their awnings and waving to the neighbors and jingling the change in their pants pockets, they chuckle with admiration to hear of his latest caper. Adult women, the mothers of our schoolmates, the divorcées, the trophies, the widows, the stepwives of our hometown, they all absolutely adore Simon—he is invited to their pools, their golf carts, their convertible Mercedes-Benz coupes.

Somehow it is understood, universally, in that way that I don't do well with—implied rather than explicit—that he is the reason our parents have divorced. Somehow it is Simon who has been fingered as the straw that has broken the back of our parents' marriage. He has been a tough kid, this much I understand, even though I don't understand it at all, what they mean by "tough." To me he is wickedly clever and outwardly fearless. He lights off a whole pack of firecrackers at once, not just one at a time, and the explosion makes your heart race and your eyes glitter. He can not only pop a wheelie but also ride it all the way down the road, across the train tracks, and take the turn where it heads into town without having to set the front wheel down. He can cup his hands together and blow into them like he's some kind of Scout leader in the front canoe on a still lake, and the low, lonesome dove whistle that comes out of his hands is, to me, magic. He stacks pennies on the train tracks to see them flattened by the local steam engine when it comes chugging by, and he only dashes away from the tracks—*chicken chicken chicken*—at the very last minute. The livid conductor pulls the whistle furiously, yelling after him as he runs off, to which Simon drops drawers and moons the guy as a final *kiss my ass*! I am so giggly proud of his clever mischief and of the way he always wins the dare. How he hides in the right corner, takes the turn just in time, shimmies up the tree, dodges the angry neighbor, outruns, outsmarts, and always, in the nick of time, evades his pursuer.

There is a weekend one summer, however, when he is forced to go downtown and wash all the police cars—as community service—because as a prank one night he is alleged to have poured a five-pound bag of sugar into the gas tank of a bull-dozer parked nearby during some routine municipal roadwork and this shifts him from Prankster to Vandal. There is some-thing scoundrelly about him, but to me he seems wily and charismatic like Spanky, innocent and humorous like Buck-wheat, and there is not one bone in his body that is criminal or malignant. In so many ways I regret that my own children, when they get to be that age, won't know such clever mischief: a carton of eggs and a can of Barbasol shaving cream and a roll of toilet paper on the night before Halloween. I regret that instead, when they get to be that age, I will excuse myself from the dinner table and cry into the kitchen sink when they casu-ally mention they had an active shooter drill at school that day. But to our mother, and to the school principal, Simon is not charmingly Mischievous. He is Distracted. Bored. Noncom-pliant. High IQ. Low attention span. He gets up to a lot of "no good." He's cutting school. Is disruptive in class. Gets terrible grades. And in a fit of wits' end she has pulled a kind of hands-in-the-air, despairing-yet-accusatory full retreat, and she has pinned the mess on our dad—*You take care of this,* she might have hissed, threateningly, *'cuz I am OUT*. Or so the common telling of the story of their divorce goes.

Our dad? He doesn't even know when our birthdays are—he always has his secretary try and remind him and even she never gets it right because he didn't know the correct in-formation to give her in the first place. So now they both—our dad and the secretary—they both forget our birthdays every year. He's the occasional-ski-trips guy who has more than once headed home at the end of a day on the slopes forgetting that he has left us at the mountain and now has to drive back to get us where we sit shivering in the parking lot. He has a famous lead foot, but also loves a glass of wine at après-ski in the lodge, so each kid has to take a shift to sit shotgun the whole ride back on Route 80, poking our dad incessantly as he starts to doze at the wheel going ninety miles per hour. *Dad! Dad! Wake up!* The parenting part of parenting is not his bag: He is the friendly you-sit-on-my-lap-and-steer-the-car-while-I-push-the-pedals type. But when cornered like that—*You take care of this, Jim!*—something else comes out of him.

Exceedingly rare, but when cornered, he has a physical temper. I only witness it twice; he once sends the entire lunchtime contents of the kitchen table clattering onto the floor with one swipe of his arm—Swiss cheese, the cutting board, the mustard jar, a jar of cornichons, crackers, the newspaper, silverware, a beer bottle, exploding across the terra-cotta tile of the kitchen in response to a thing my mother has said. And another time, someone has helped themselves to the forbidden foil packets of dark chocolate that our mother hides in the depths of certain kitchen drawers for herself. And when she is standing there with her wooden spoon in hand, demanding to know which one of us has gotten their little *filthy fingers* into her things, it's possible that I have not bravely come forward, and it's possible that she has blamed Simon and that Simon— who is now our dad's problem, apparently—has taken the hit. Our dad, our charismatic, romantic, softhearted, watercolor-painting, daddy-o dad, feeling cornered by my mother, has grabbed Simon by the face, squeezing his cheeks so hard he makes a fish mouth. *You want some chocolate? You want some chocolate?* And starts shoving what's left of the foil packets into his tears-and-snot-slobbered mouth. It's possible Simon is regularly and wrongly scapegoated, and has possibly never felt that great about me, his stupid little sister, with her habit of fishing around in off-limits drawers and helping herself to what she finds there, while he takes the fall.

I AM GETTING off at the end of the night from my new job washing dishes. I have walked back home from town in the dark under the black-silhouetted canopy of trees. The houselights are on. The crickets blast. The cicadas swell and crescendo. I see the dark outline of The Car. My Car.

It is not parked in the brightly lit driveway but is tucked in at the top of the street, in dark stealth, up by our mailbox. Simon is upstairs in the shower and his clothes are in a pile in the hallway. I creep up those steep stairs, a cat on all fours, dig through the pockets, find the car key, and whoosh silently back downstairs, through the kitchen, past the two beautiful vintage Chicago Cutlery knives—washed, dried, laid out on the old worn cutting board like *objets*—and run up the hill to the car to reclaim what is rightfully mine. As Simon lathers and shampoos in the shower, I drive away. I roll-start her in second gear, with the headlights off until I get a good distance from the house, and with a giddy righteous vengeance pounding in my heart I accidentally blast the high beams and shift into third. There's a party at the Hansens' and even though I haven't been invited, I'm going.

I REFUSE TO say I'm the stupidest of the bunch. I'm not technically stupid—but I'm not the one in the family who got accepted to Mensa, or the one who had the IQ test that made the school counselor call our parents for a meeting, or the one who graduated from a top-tier school. I will concede that there is a dull part of my brain, where I still live in the cotton of my own mind. I'm the one who thought it would be a victory to steal back a stolen car for a second time. I was not thinking long-term strategic win or overall decisive victory. Just: *There's the car!* Just: *You fucker, Simon!* Just: *I want back what is rightfully mine.* I just wanted to strike and win in the moment, and before I could even think it through, I was going through his pockets, hunting for the key, and driving off, like a moth seduced by the glowing flame of Justice. Even though it was not the smartest move, I understand my thinking at the time, as if we were simply in a bigger, more high-stakes game of freeze tag or prisoner tag, and all was fair play. Even in the moment I am certain I am within bounds, and I have the giddy sense that everything is now Even Steven. We will simply gather back at the tree stump and start counting off for the next round.

But when I finally get home with the car, Simon is there waiting, fuming, jumpy, like a horse in a thunderstorm. He is also drunk. And then, as if there has been a crack of lightning across the sky and the barn door has been blown off its hinges, he rears up and lunges at me. He starts by yanking me across the front yard by my neck and hair through the pachysandra. Then he is raking me across the gravel. Then he is dragging me by the leg down the two shallow steps made from thick railroad ties; I smell their reek of creosote as I go down and feel the hot road rash on my spine. My clothes are stained, things are going fast. Violence is a quick and hot thing, and I suspect we are both now numb from the blistering white heat of it. It

has a very short lifespan but it is explosive. I don't know if
I am screaming or silent; both are possible. He drops my
ankle and strides purposefully to the kitchen screen door
just beyond which those knives are laid artfully on the
table—Chicago Cutlery, wood handles, brass pins, carbon
steel blades—and in a surge of adrenal rush before he can get
back and start slashing me to ribbons, I scramble up, out of
the trampled pachysandra, and run and run and run, lungs
burning, cicadas swelling and crescendoing, out our back
meadow, along the stream, across the railroad tracks, then
along the back roads for the next several hours, sometimes
stopping dead to catch my breath, to listen for sounds of pursuit. Convinced it is him behind the wheel of a lone approach-
ing car, coming after me to finish me off, I dive into the thick
weeded ditch by the side of the road to avoid the oncoming
headlights. And then I walk until I get back to the Hansens'
house and day is breaking.

I finally get the guts up to sneak into our house some days
later to leave a note for my dad so he can find me when he gets
home from the city. *I've been staying at the Hansens'. I can
explain everything. Only call when you are calm and ready to
talk.*

Who am I writing that note to? What imagined father do I
have in my fictionalizing mind? A father who will shout, *Go to
your room! You are grounded for the rest of your life!* A father
who will storm in, storm out, rattle the cage. A father who
will stride into his own house in need of a blanket and yell up
the stairs at his soon-to-be ex-wife, *Give me a fucking blanket,
you insufferable bitch!* and not stand passively at the threshold
of it, shoulders hunched, explaining his situation to his ten-
year-old daughter doing dishes; a father who will bring order

to the court. A father who needs to be calmed down before we can talk.

But that is not the father I have.

He does his work on you, for sure, when he finds you displeasing, but he is more of a scathing "doozy" man, what we call his Real Doozies—these savage things he sometimes says, not directly to you but about you. Pointedly declared when you are within earshot. We hold our hands over our mouths to cover the scandalized laughter it draws out in us, like when you hear a filthy, depraved joke. He gets his work done, but he is not your thundering wooden-spoon type.

My dad has read the note, called the house where I am hiding out, and has decided we should have lunch, out at a restaurant, like two grown and equal people. Like I'm a client or a potential candidate for a job. He's taking me to an old tavern upriver called Colligan's Stockton Inn. It's always been a special-occasion place for our family. The bartender would make us kids Shirley Temples, and they used to have a Saint Bernard so big I could ride it like a pony.

We sit outside near the wishing well, made famous in a Rodgers and Hart song with a chorus that goes "There's a small hotel with a wishing well." We order crab cakes and salads, and for him, "just two fingers of whatever white you have open"; he is cordial with the waiter but not welcoming him into our personal private meeting—not today, not this bar crowd, not this dinner party, not this funny story. His thirteen-year-old daughter has backed his car out of the family driveway and has been joyriding it all over the county. So today there is a certain gravitas as we are seated at his regular table—we are two calm adults at a business lunch discussing The Confidential Project, The Proprietary Proposal, The Overbudget Budget.

"It wasn't mine to take but it wasn't his, either!" I explain.

"He was drunk!" I tattle.

My famously center-stage father quietly sips his wine; he is not interrupting, not telling his own stories, certainly not yelling. He is hearing me out, giving me all the room and as much time as I need. He doesn't agree or disagree, just focuses, looking down at his lap, listening.

"And look at this!" I say, untucking my shirt.

In the garden with the bubbling wishing well, where we sit on the white wrought iron patio furniture, with the gazebo overhead, and the remains of crab and salad on our plates, I show my dad the bruises on my legs, the carpet of scabbed-over road rash all along my back. I feel I have exactingly explained the whole situation and will obviously be forgiven, now that we have a clearer understanding of what has transpired and how it happened, but after a lengthy pause, my dad clears his throat and says:

"Well. It's a good thing it wasn't me, because if I'd been home, I would've finished the job." And he waves to the waiter for our check.

Clearing his throat again, signaling that Our Contract Is Ready for Signatures, Our Business Dealings Are Concluding, my dad says, "As for Simon, he has strict instructions not to lay a hand on you. I want you back in the house by this afternoon."

I DO COME back to the house. And yet I find it empty and myself again alone in it. My dad has gone right back to work and is as buried as ever. A few days later I'm walking along the narrow corridor back to my room from having a shower, wrapped in my towel, and I startle to see Simon for the first time since the beatdown, coming up the stairs. I force myself to coolly keep step in spite of the urge to freeze, and as I stonily pass him, without speaking, he violently jerks his hand back as if to bludgeon me; I flinch wildly, and then— "Psych!!!!"—he drops his arm, loose as a cooked strand of spaghetti, and continues past me to his room, leaving me untouched, but full-tilt adrenal. I can't settle down. For weeks my heart races as if I have been sprinting, even when I am alone and sitting still. And that's the end of him, as far as I'm concerned.

We become two members of the family, one brother and one sister, who can no longer be in the same room together, but who will find strange ways nonetheless to be in the same room together when we must. There is no one here who finds it necessary to marshal us to a satisfactory peace. So we, as young teenagers, broker our own strange unspoken détente, one that leaves us both in a peculiar kind of solitary confinement in which we share yard privileges with the general population—while our family goes on about its business. There will be Thanksgivings and Christmases up ahead, for a few more years at least, and we two out of the gang will just sit at opposite ends of those tables, have a drink in one room while the other is having an hors d'oeuvre in the other, as we commence our lifetime's careful orchestration of being two members of an otherwise operating family who are now left to disapprove of each other in isolation. He is not in my *I will never ever speak to you again* category, but for the next forty years, I will speak to him only a handful of times. If I needed to track him down, I would have to ask somebody for his address, and the same for him—if he needed to get ahold of me, he would be obliged to find someone who knows my phone number.

Not that we have yet had any occasion to do so.

MAD MONEY

BEFORE HE STARTED having *gals* and *dames* and the elaborate dinner parties for which he will soon gain a reputation, when anyone asked me how my dad had been holding up since the divorce, I'd find myself in a grimace of concern and a real grief in my heart—*Oh, my poor dad. I think he still loves my mom. Poor guy.* I ached for him.

He took it hard and did not bounce right back.

But then, when he does start to recover, he flourishes.

He is no longer wounded; there are no more winsome love duets on cassettes in the Walkman. He is fresh milk, frothy; I can't count how many times I hear him now referred to as "a real renaissance man." He is dating ladies he gives nicknames to, by which he exclusively refers to them:

The Well-Digger's Daughter
The Firecracker

The Hum and Strum
The Horse Breeder
The Contessa

I like all of them, very much, with their vivacious and sparkling personalities, but at first I am startled to come downstairs in the mornings to find some stranger rummaging around in the refrigerator looking for an egg, who then, after we've introduced ourselves, decides she wants to talk to me like I'm a roommate with whom she might discuss last night's events. I feel this terrible, oily awkwardness in my chest and instantly carburate it to a fine and smooth-burning mist of feigned indifference, and she doesn't catch on. She just hunts for bread to toast, and I shrug apologetically that we don't have any. But he's really starting to come back to life. He's seeing the world, taking himself on the vacations he was not free to take when we were kids. Has booked a trip on the *QE II*. He sits on the deck under a blanket, sketches a little in the mornings, and allows himself a nap in the afternoons. They bring him a cup of hot clam broth or beef bouillon when it gets chilly on deck and even though he criticizes the food as "undistinguished" and the broth as "from a can," he thinks the gesture is *sensational;* he is impressed that even out on the deck they serve your hot bouillon on monogrammed china.

His own cooking is becoming ambitious. He now wears a kerchief around his neck, a striped apron over his dress shirt, and he expertly drapes a kitchen towel over his shoulder as he trusses capons and flips crêpes suzette into the air. He is cultivating his expression of Beauty: "diamonds and burlap," as he calls it. It is a careful blend of high and low culture, by which he means he admires mastery of craft and respects high-quality work, but he can't stand pretentiousness, and he espe-cially derides things he finds too *precious*. He skewers any person with *chi-chi* affectations or *la-di-da* mannerisms by pretending to dab at the corners of his cartoonishly pursed mouth, pinkies out, with an implied white napkin.

Forget anyone who walks into an ice cream parlor asking for *butter pecaaaahn*. The half-gallon tub he has stashed in his own freezer?

Mint. Chip.

He is not one for the symphony or the ballet or driving into nearby Princeton to attend academic lectures; instead, he has taken up tap dancing with two of his best friends, and once a week they drive downriver for lessons in Trenton. Trenton is the state capital, the county seat, and the home of pork roll, oyster crackers, Bayer aspirin, Magic Markers, and heavy manu-facturing: steel, brick, porcelain, iron, wire, and cable. In co-lossal letters on the bridge that spans the Delaware River, the city declares its pride: TRENTON MAKES, THE WORLD TAKES. Which Jeffrey wisecracks about. "What the World Refuses, Trenton Uses!" Our father was born in Trenton.

And now he finds himself reborn—*renaissance man*—by going to tap classes there. They stop for dinner afterward at Chick and Nello's, in the Chambersburg neighborhood, where guys in tracksuits sit at the bar nursing shot glasses of Fernet-Branca. We find this colorful and story-worthy, but it's what's on their plates that really lights my father up—a few blistered peppers, salted, doused in olive oil. A cup of tortellini in brodo. A simply roasted breast of veal.

He throws parties all the time now, not just our annual summer lamb roasts but weeknight dinners and New Year's Day lunches and paella parties and Easter brunches. He's got one lined up for after his first tap dance recital, in a few weeks. It'll be to celebrate all of their dedicated work, all of that rehearsing with their top hats and their black canes, but more than anything, it's a good excuse for another dinner party. They'll be doing a little choreographed bit, and their names will be listed on the program next to the eight-year-old girls doing their ballet routines, and the teenagers in crisp pairs showing off their waltzes and tangos. He is delighted at the tongue-in-cheek of this, the three middle-aged men doing a little "number," ironically, self-consciously. They have their bow ties and tuxedoes ready; they have their patent leather lace-up tap shoes, and they'll consider themselves lucky if they hit even half of their marks. "But that's not the point," he says. "It's all for the yuks of it." And for the party to follow, in their honor.

MEANWHILE, IT'S BEEN a slow, unproductive, often chaotic number of years for Jeffrey. Ever since he came back from Africa it seems to have all stalled for him, and momentum is hard for him to hold steady. He can never make it to the bank on time. Can't get his truck to start. Always has a broken crown or a toothache, is always having a conflict with an old friend, a problem with rent, with organizing his time. He has to stack the wood, or clear out the garage, or sweep the barn in the dark, by the headlights of his truck, because, well, that very morning he had to have some breakfast of course and then "well, a complete shower, with flossing," he explains, which can take up to ninety minutes, he insists, and then on the way to the hardware store he ran into a friend he hadn't seen in quite a while and they started talking and gradually, unplanned events stack up on other happenstance events until he has been delayed all the daylight hours, and evening has set in when he finally arrives to the job he has been hired to do that morning.

These are the emerging eccentricities that make Jeffrey Jeffrey, which we in his surrounding orbit find charming, hilarious, sometimes exasperating but mostly entertaining; and the details of which we all quickly fold into our admiration. With mirth and amiable teasing, we recount these quirky anecdotes to others:

A *complete shower!*
Ninety minutes to also floss!
He can split and stack a whole cord of wood in the dark, by moonlight!

We find him so amusing. So special. So charismatic. With the pointed exception of our dad. About Jeffrey, whenever anyone asks after him and how he's doing, our dad makes a wincing face as if the question itself is a foul odor—the water in a vase of week-old flowers. He then gathers himself and forces a smile and says, "Well, he does his best . . ." He holds up his hands as if he has no explanation and wants nothing to do with the matter. He does not make an effort to hide his distaste, his disrespect, and it soon becomes understood all around our small town that Jeffrey and our dad "have their issues."

But then Jeffrey, too, starts to turn it around. After a few fits and starts at community college and a state school, getting some of his requirements in order, he applies to and gets into Stanford. Moves to California. He struggles with the scene in Palo Alto. Tangles at times with his roommates. Loves only his Arabic professor, but otherwise feels fed up with what he describes as "children teaching students." He flubs his introductory geology class requirement, which costs him a whole additional expensive semester, and ultimately decides he hates "the game" of anthropology, after all. Instead he plans to intern at a local newspaper because he "still loves People and Writing about them," as he says in his neatly folded typewritten letters home to our mom, in Vermont. But nonetheless, he has conquered Academia, and soon he will graduate. The fact of his finally getting through college—and such a prestigious one—in spite of the ninety-minute showers and the constant scramble for cash and the difficulty organizing his time reinforces my idea of him as extra potent. Exceptional. And endorses him, at least in my mind, as highly competent. Perhaps eccentric, yes, but in our family's syntax individuality is highly prized; to be special, unique, and not like everybody else is our whole gestalt. We grew up in the burned-out ruins of a silk mill with pigeons warbling in the stone walls, not in one of the tidy new construction sites up the way with identical front doors and mailboxes. Everybody went "down the shore" for summer vacation, but my mother "would not be caught dead at the Jersey Shore"; we were taken instead to far-flung places no one has heard of: Ajaccio, Bénodet, Split. When we drive a country road and come upon the powerful stink of a startled skunk, our mother urgently has us all roll the windows down, not up—"Smell that!" she insists, taking deep ecstatic inhales, and exhorting us to do the same. To be contrarian is respectable, but somehow Jeffrey, with his distinguishing idiosyncrasies—his trash-hauling business and his top-drawer education—a pitch-perfect "diamonds and burlap" embodiment of our father's ideal of Beauty, nonetheless does not elicit admiration or kind regard from our father. Rather, our dad seems threatened. He sighs heavily, tries to disguise his displeasure as good humor, always makes the joke in public at Jeff's expense: *I spent eighty thousand dollars on his education and he hauls trash for a living!*

The son's graduation is the same weekend as the father's tap dance recital.

I AM SEVENTEEN years old and living in New York City at this time. I've somehow skipped ninth and eleventh grade and have already finished high school. After a tenuous first semester at NYU, I've tanked. I'm a college dropout cocktail waitress in a huge downtown club making a lot of money. I've lied about my age to get the job, and I'm also skimming from the house; it's a little felony hustle everybody who works there is in on, and they have taken me under their wing, taught me the scam. We "cash and carry" our own banks and sell cocktails that our bartenders never ring up, then we split the take. My sister is my roommate, finishing art school, in spite of a lifetime of having our father put two fingers to his temple and pull his thumb as the trigger whenever she expressed her wish to be a painter. He has joked her whole life about cutting her hands off at the wrists—"Cut 'em off!" he quips; it's his stock advice to any of his friends whose own children show talent as artists. As if it were a fate worse than death to be an artist, and as if she is already destined to a failure he, with his discerning eye, has predicted with flat certainty. But what comes from her hands is hardly mediocre. Even as early as grade school she has won the still life prizes and they have hung her work in the halls of the elementary school building, right outside the principal's office. There I paused so many days and looked up at it admiringly—her artful composition of the green wine bottle and the wobbly misshapen lemon and the midnight-blue tabletop—my own big sister already drawn to the Rothko color fields, even in sixth grade—with the chalky blues and the smokey yellows and the dense, nearly black greens. She makes me for my thirteenth birthday a watercolor painting—cubist—of a layered birthday cake, a mosaic of loose, bleeding cubes, stacked upon each other, and somehow, with just her incredible hands and the brushes kept in their dirty coffee cans spread out on newspaper, somehow she has imbued feelings into the frame; it is a seemingly simple object—a layered birthday cake with flickering candles—but it's nothing like her classmates' rigid and unimaginative anatomical renderings of horses with shiny manes, and this painting somehow emanates bittersweetness, excitement, and a slight melancholy.

She doesn't know about the cash-and-carry hustle I'm involved in, but she is alarmed at the cocaine and the tequila I consume. In our family she is famously moderate, responsible, almost prudish. My mother in Vermont knows nothing about either, and she is preoccupied with her own worry about money, and so this is the year I've taken on my mother's heating fuel and utility bills as a Christmas present; I send her cashier's checks. It's the right thing to do, and she accepts it, but it's fraught. Her reticence to accept the gift is palpable; her need to accept it, also palpable.

My dad, meanwhile, is delighted at how well I'm doing for myself and doesn't question it. He has always been enamored with people who have money on hand, at the ready, cash in pocket, money to burn, *front money, mattress money*—he loves that—and I am now in the habit of carrying an actual roll, secured with a rubber band, as one of the waitresses at the club taught me to do, so that it would be held securely twisted under the waistband of my stockings and always in reach, to pat, to check on, to account for. You do not want to duck into the bathroom stall to blow a few lines in the middle of your shift and then go back out to your station only to realize your cash has scooched its way out of a back pocket and dropped onto the floor and someone has grabbed it, *finders keepers*. Whenever there's an opportunity, I pull out my roll, peel off bills for the cabbie or the coat check, and I see my dad grin at me each time. His seventeen-year-old daughter riding high.

WHAT'S OUR FAVORITE movie around this time? His and mine?

Paper Moon.

We share a swooning admiration for charming grifters. We are both besotted by ten-year-old girls who act like fifty-year-old con men, and we revere the clever con. We chuckle at Addie in *Paper Moon,* a ten-year-old who can smoke cigarettes and drive a stick shift. We love the father-daughter swindle, and he jokes that we could get our own little hustle going, that we would be a perfect team; I could be the bait, the innocent young girl who brings the mark in, and he could play the straight man, while I pick the pockets, rig the deck of cards, forge the signature, charge twenty-four dollars for the counterfeit engraved Bible. He would love to be able to tell *that* story at one of his dinner parties. Even my stealing of the car a few years before has become one of his favorite family yarns, recounted now with a chuckling pride. He loves a rascal. I love to be his rascal.

But now he and I have a conflict: his tap dance recital on the very same weekend as Jeff's graduation. And my dad's not going to the graduation; he is instead going through with his recital. I call my father routinely, to catch up and check in and have a joke, and he keeps in regular touch with me, too, but now I'm calling to tell him, adult-to-adult, man-to-man, that it's a bad decision.

"Gabbies, hey!" He puts the phone to his chest, turns to whoever is in the office with him at the time. "It's New York calling!" he tells them. Then he quips to them, "She must need money. They only call when they need money!" and I hear laughter all around in the background.

I've been on my own for long enough by now, making my own money, that we both know that this is a fiction of his—a punch line—but I good-naturedly wait until the laughter dies down, and he returns the phone to his ear. I feel like a grown adult who has to have a stern word with her own father. And I hear myself say:

"Well, Dad, I just think you should be attending your first son's graduation." My voice communicates a patient, matter-of-fact parental firmness toward a child; I give him the *Sorry, Charlie* treatment, like I'm the one in charge, insisting there will be no dessert until the broccoli has been eaten.

"I just think you should be there for Jeffrey's hard-won ac-complishment." This seventeen-year-old's opinion delivered with shrugged-shoulder stonewalling, as if to say, *It's up to you, kiddo, but I don't think this is your best effort.* He starts clearing his throat as he does when he's nervous. Or furious.

He has come to love the life of our small "shitkicker" town, as he lovingly calls it. Perhaps in response to having been ultimately outmatched by the big city, having lost money yet again on yet another doomed show, he has given up the stage and theater work that used to take him to New York and is now designing private homes and remodels and shopping plazas in our area, and he is really hunkering down in it, becoming especially fond of stewarding his own community, where he was raised, where he raised his own. He takes it seriously and has sat on the planning commission and on city council and on the boards of various arts organizations, but he is always referring to himself and his small-town life in the diminutive. He uses words like "shitkicker" and "our little neck of the woods." Or sometimes he calls it Hobbitsville. When he leaves messages for me on my answering machine he'll say, "Hello, New York! It's Hobbitsville, here. Just saying hello." And there is always a hint of something in his tone, at the back of his voice in those messages, a kind of envy. Sarcasm. And an admonishment, as if to say, *Don't get ahead of yourself, little missy.*

On the weekend that his son Jeffrey will graduate from college, it is also true, and apparently unsolvable, that his daughter Melissa will graduate from college. An unfortunate double landing of two airplanes that should have had staggered arrivals but, because of Jeff's early tribulations, and a couple of Melissa's as well, for whatever reasons, they are both having important milestones on the same weekend. Could this have been worked out? Yes, of course. Everybody was thinking creatively about the two graduations on the same weekend. Yet this third problem, his tap dance recital, remains non-negotiable. "You know, Gabs, it's too late for me to back out. I've already got a whole crowd coming to the show that weekend."

"I really think you should be going to California, Dad."

He says he can't make it to any of the graduation ceremonies, but he has had the idea to just combine his recital and Melissa's reception and make one big festive party celebrating the both of them.

"I don't know, Dad," I press on, heavy skepticism in my voice. "I think that's going to be really saying something to Jeffrey." And before I realize it, I have cornered him. The kind of corner that makes him a different man.

"Sonuvabitch!" He hangs up the phone on me, turning me now into his adversary and no longer his co-conspirator Bible salesman.

A little later he's gathered himself and calls back. He pivots from *can't go* to *can't afford to go*. He's broke. It's too expensive.

"I don't have that kind of money right now, Gabs. I just don't have it. I don't know what to tell ya."

THIS IS AN old problem for him and isn't untrue. He's a wreck with money, always has been. Always short, in the hole, up all night unable to sleep, nails bitten to their nubs, his sheets and white T-shirts have big Dalmatian stains of black ink from the felt-tip pens that drop to his chest when he finally dozes off at three A.M. with the crossword puzzle propped against his knees, the bedside lamp blazing. And yet, if he wants champagne on the Christmas table, he'll find the cash for that even if he has to siphon gas for the car. He has let the electricity get cut off at our house, but he makes it to Aspen for deep-powder spring skiing. He loves the language of money, the theater of money, the power of money, but just can never make enough of it or carefully allocate any of it. He orders booklets of uncut dollar bills from the Franklin Mint and makes a big Vaudevillian to-do of licking his thumb then tearing them off one by one to hand to doormen and taxi drivers and coat check girls when he makes holiday trips into New York. "Glove Money," he calls it. He can explain how he covered payroll by pulling delinquency on our school tuition. "Sometimes you gotta rob Peter to pay Paul," he shrugs, smiling puckishly. "And everybody eventually got paid and everybody went to college in the end, right?" he grins.

You, too, will shrug and grin about his funny juggling of money. You, too, will smile puckishly when telling the story about how, once in high school and once in college, you find yourself locked out of your assigned housing, with a letter in your campus mailbox letting you know that you have been administratively withdrawn. You've arrived with your quilt and your jar of coins, your lava lamp and your boxes. You go down to the bursar's office to negotiate, but no explanation or plea will open the room door, so you have to leave campus, to scramble, to sleep in the back of a friend's station wagon in the parking lot for a few days while your dad "robs Peter."

"It's shortsighted to let money be the reason you don't do something you can't afford!" he loves to say.

It's from him that I learned how to kite a check with the

new ATM machines that were springing up when automated banking first started really catching on; if you needed a little cash advance for the weekend, you could deposit an empty envelope after four P.M. on Friday, receive cash back, and return to the bank on Monday during business hours to innocently and with profuse apology make good on your "mistake." He used to make great charming ceremony of suavely pressing a five-dollar bill in my hand as I ran off to Little League practice: "Here, Gabbies, a little Mad Money, just in case." And later, at the car wash or the soft-serve ice cream place, he'd ask for it back.

I don't know what Mad Money is, I'm nine, I play third base, I had begged to quit ballet so I could play baseball, and he explains, "A father slips his daughter a little 'Mad Money' as she is heading out on a date, in case the date gets fresh with her, and she needs cab fare home." I have heard about "getting fresh" before but only as a threat from a parent to a child that has dared to talk back, never in this context, between two adults on a date. I am thrilled by this new meaning and the pictures it brings up in my imagination, a man and a woman in a car, out on a bluff, at night. And she is pissed off, but she luckily has money in her pocket, and is therefore free—she can storm off and hail a cab. Mad Money!

DURING OUR YEAR in Vermont in the midst of my parents' divorce, my progressive school had a class trip to New York City with plans to visit a famous artist's studio and also to meet a famous poet, and by incredible luck, my dad was doing a show there at the same time; we would get to visit him at work. I could show my classmates what a theater looked like during load-in: stage doors, loading docks, green rooms, the wings. I could explain to them about Local 829, and the proper way to say IATSE, which you pronounce like the board game Yahtzee, and the PAR cans and the scrims and the gels and the catwalks and the barn doors and the union time clocks and the rigging—all of the things we used to see on paper in his roller rink office, I will get to show it all off to my new Vermont schoolmates. We took the long overnight train from Montpelier, and when we arrived in Penn Station, I was giddy with excitement. But it was, yet again, a terribly produced musical that never even made it past opening night of previews and the money to finance the production was "lousy" money, he explained.

That doomed Broadway show, he used to tell the story of it years later at his dinner parties, had runners coming in the backstage door and dropping paper lunch bags to the director and producer, who sat in the orchestra seats during rehearsals. Drug money, in cash, he implied. It made a great yarn at the dinner table—lively, colorful, slightly louche.

But in real time, when I'm on my seventh-grade field trip from Vermont to New York City, we have all walked up Eighth Avenue to the Majestic Theatre, and when we get into the theater, we are seven excited, jittering adolescents, all of us damp from a freak spring snow flurry. The mood in the room is not colorful or lively or louche; it's grim. I haven't seen him since being taken to Vermont with our mother; I am juiced. Between the hammering pulse of the city and the grand theater itself—an actual Broadway house, with balcony seating, a ceiling so tall your heart fills with awe and floats up to the rafters—it may as well be a great cathedral.

He's down in front, standing and facing the proscenium; we've filed in at the back, taken over those rows at the top of the ramp where the ushers will stand like sentinels with flashlights for latecomers. The room lights are on and a tech platform like one of those floating docks in a lake is still set up over a section of middle seats in the orchestra—they have not moved their operation up to the booth yet, with headsets and whispering; they are still early in running tech rehearsals. There are no actors onstage, just stagehands and electricians.

Board operators are calling out cues and making adjustments over the loudspeakers like a sound check before a concert—it's thrilling, but even I can see they are terribly behind schedule. Someone goes to tell him we are here, and he remains where he is, doing what he is doing—talking to a stagehand.

Eventually he breaks away and walks up the corridor toward us, then he recognizes me out of the group of kids I'm with, and his eyes turn from distracted and preoccupied to a deadly hollow, the little signal to show he despises—and fears—this interruption. *Oh, that's just great. I'm in the middle of getting a fucking show off the ground and now you're here?* is what they say to me, his eyes. But out of his mouth comes a long, starchy, "Heeeeeey. Gabeez." He clears his throat, makes a strained effort to smile over what's already plainly written on his face. He's conspicuously slow about it, as if some part of him wishes to be sure you will see and take note that he is mustering. It's not his fault, but in doing so he has created, for me, a terrible confusion of blurry rubouts and smudges, like a practice math sheet rife with mistakes sloppily gone over with a dirty eraser. Now the new, correct answers are scratched in their places—he is technically smiling—but is that a three or an eight? Is he loving or loathing? I don't think it should be his problem that I read faces so acutely, but I do think he should remember this about me by now and make some effort. He's had twelve years to get to know me.

Our perceptive seventh-grade teacher immediately sees what's happening, introduces himself to my dad, and promises,

"We won't take any of your time,"

says he is

"So grateful for the opportunity, the kids are thrilled just to even be here, please please don't let us take you away from your business."

My dad seems unable to relinquish his irritability over the intrusion I've already perpetrated upon him, but when he realizes we will be on our way in just a few minutes and won't be needing anything from him, he relents a little and addresses the others in the group with a generous concern: "You guys all have a place to stay?"

He reaches into his pocket to give me some money, but he only has a twenty and a mini emery board—he's trying to stop being a nailbiter, he says—and he wants to give me a five; he asks me if I have any change. We do a bit of shuffling in our pockets and backpacks, and it takes a few minutes as he stands in row 23 and I stand in row 24, trying to make change for him so that I can get the twenty and he can keep the sixteen I have in exchange. It's the most expensive four dollars I have ever earned. And then we pack ourselves up and head back out into the fluke spring snow shower, on to the artist's studio, and the poet's house, and then back to Vermont.

BUT WHETHER HE has a legitimate scheduling conflict given the double graduation or he can't afford a ticket to California, this commitment to the tap dance recital strikes me as a declaration, a signal he is signaling. And I'm not the only one in this family who tunes in to faces, gestures, messages, moods: I worry for Jeffrey.

"Wait a minute. Wait a minute, Dad. Now you're saying you're not going to Jeffrey's graduation because you don't have the money?" I am unrelenting.

He clears his throat. "I can't swing it, Gabs."

As soon as we hang up, I call my brother Todd. Todd is solid money, quality money. He's the Mensa-at-sixteen guy, the one who graduated from high school in Wales with an international baccalaureate, who made honors on the dean's list every semester at Skidmore College, and who followed that up with a stint at the Berklee College of Music before he became the Wall Street guy he is when I call him about this graduation problem. At the time, Todd is twenty-four years old and has made a splash in the trade papers because he's the youngest vice president Goldman Sachs has ever had. He's the only guy in our family with Reliable Money. And he hasn't yet dropped dead from a rare and massive stroke, an explosion in his carotid artery one afternoon after years of ignored sleep apnea. Oh, *by the way,* as my dad would say, cueing up the delivery of one of his buried ledes, I should mention that we have another dead brother. But for now, he's very alive and he has Quality Money and he's the one I call immediately.

"Dad says he can't afford to go to Jeff's graduation," I tell him. "Will you split it with me if I get him a round-trip ticket?"

"Yeah, I agree. That's effed up. If he wanted to go, he could find a way to go." I'm not alone among the siblings; it is common knowledge that Jeff is our father's bête noire. Todd says he'll buy the ticket to California.

I call my dad back and announce my triumph: "I got you a ticket."

I'm so thrilled at my win—not only telling the man what the right thing to do is, and instructing him on the right father to be, but also footing the bill. I don't see it coming, his outrage. "Sonuvabitch!" he spits into the phone. He is out of the car—so to speak—and hailing a cab. My smug, seventeen-year-old sassing back, this "getting fresh" with my father, does something to him, and then, irrevocably, to us. He refuses the plane ticket, does not attend the graduation, and brings down the house at the tap dance recital. They print his smiling picture in the *Trenton Times*. For years to follow, he won't make eye contact with me. Mad Money.

SILVER LINING

So, TODD. The first dead brother.

T-Bone. Loader. Loader Bone. Alive in the morning, dead in the afternoon, two months shy of his forty-sixth birthday.

I'm in New York, I've opened a restaurant, recently broken up with a long-term girlfriend, and have even more recently—surprisingly—married an Italian man, eleven years my senior.

Unpredictability, impermanence, upheaval, tumult—I traffic in all of it. "Show me one person who doesn't lead a complicated life," I am fond of saying around this time. I'm thirty-eight years old and thirty-eight weeks pregnant with our first child when my sister, in New Jersey, calls with the dreadful news of Todd. I'm the chef, not just the owner, so even though I'm huge, short of breath, and having to pee every hour, I'm still butchering at the stainless-steel prep table, still waddling about from the burners to the sink to the walk-in refrigerator or to pick up the phone in the office with my apron tied up—empire style—around my rib cage.

"Gabs, hi. Sorry. I have some news about Todd. He's in the hospital, in a coma, and they can see the extent of the damage and they don't see any chance, but he's on life support; she has to make a decision within twenty-four hours—we've asked her to hold off until we all can get out there."

"She" refers to Todd's wife, who is sitting there with the plug in her hand, churning with the decision to pull it or not. Except it turns out it is not her decision to make at all— California law says when you are brain dead for twenty-four hours, you are dead dead.

"I don't know, Meliss," I say, disbelieving that it is as grave as it sounds, and hoping to add some clear-eyed reasonableness to the situation.

"I feel like he could wake up. You know Todd; he's so healthy. Not to mention controlling!" I joke.

"Give it a couple hours and let's see," I say.

We agree to check in a little later and hang up. I call my obstetrician, who forbids me to fly; she's expecting me to go into labor any day.

Todd had, many years earlier, decamped to sunny California, having cashed out of his high-octane Wall Street career in "the big worm"—as he delighted in calling New York City. His sarcastic assessment of the city, with its crushing pace and pressure, was that it was not the big juicy apple that young ambitious people famously took big bites out of while conquering, but rather it was like a long burrowing invertebrate that bored through you and hollowed you out, both morally and psychically. So, he quit while he was ahead. He'd taken his significant earnings, his young family, and moved out West.

But even in breezy California, the land of fresh bay leaves and long afternoons, where he can mountain bike from his very doorstep out and up into the hills surrounding his house in San Anselmo, even here he organizes his days with strict precision and requires the same of his family, keeps his appointments punctually, demands the same of others, keeps his phone calls focused and terse, rehearses with his band on a regimented schedule, and even here, surrounded by fresh eucalyptus whose dangling branches tenderly brush against the windows at night, Todd does not sleep well and hasn't for years.

He doesn't feel the need to whine about it or have it checked out. This is a shared characteristic in the family—we do not tend to over-pamper ourselves. He'd run a marathon with a headache. And on the next day, he woke up with the same headache, worsened. He decided to take a nap to see if it would help but woke up from that nap with the headache now even stronger, and at the insistence of his wife, finally took himself to the ER. Hearing his complaint that his vision in his right eye reminded him of the digitally blurred images used to protect the identity of someone as seen on TV shows, they quickly ordered a CT angiogram. While on the table in the scan, he suffered a massive explosion in the carotid artery, perhaps associated—some think—with his unattended-to sleep apnea. A rare and undetected acute angle in one of the long blue arterial ribbons that threaded from his heart to his brain had gotten kinked up, just behind his ear, and ripped open. He was brain-dead in the moment, then dead dead the next day, when they pulled the plug, reducing us from five brothers and sisters to four.

The day before, he'd been a father of three preteen children.

The day before he'd been a husband of seventeen years. The day before, he'd been healthy, fit, sound of mind and body, drug-free, musically gifted, financially organized—if anything, as my father used to say about him, wrinkling up into a squint of distaste, "a little too Straight and Narrow, no?" But to me, a disciplined, successful, rational, and highly prized crewmate. To me, the most reliable and the most versatile—with his astute and empathic right-brain function and his swift, highly accurate left-brain function. With him you only had to say the first few words, and he understood immediately where you were headed, whether you were talking about a plane ticket or a poem, and he met you there, immediately. Also, he sought pleasure. He laughed. His contagious, relaxing laugh. A high-pitched, joyous-yet-reprimanding, judgmental-yet-affectionate, hooting, gleeful hee-hee-hee-hee-hee-hee, followed by "No shit, Sherlock!" At even the things he was chapped by. Even stupidity, inefficiency, illogic, dullness of mind, slowness of response, wasted opportunity, hypocrisy, self-delusion—he answered all with bright and exuberant and forgiving laughter. Man's eternal, persistent foolishness: Todd's greatest source of incredulous delight.

I digested the news of my brother's sudden death as if it was an exhilarating story, the story of a freak accident. I hung up from the phone call, put my head down on my desk at the restaurant, broke open for ten seconds when I realized he was not coming back, that even he was not type-A enough to control this—but then I got up and waddled back to work, still in my apron. Had my baby a few days later.

I had liked Todd very much and saved his voice messages and contact in my phone for years and years to follow, but I didn't unduly mourn or extravagantly grieve his death because

I understood it, and to understand something is to have no argument with it. To have no argument is to be spared an immense portion of grief—not the whole of it, but the otherwise all-consuming futile portion of grief that one could spend demanding of the swirling, vaporous universe: *Why? Why him?* But in this instance, the answer was so reasonable and so immediately available: *Why not? Why not him? Why not any of us?* He'd simply been one of those random ones who are taken too soon, too young, from no apparent misstep of his own. It was comprehensible and indisputable. For years to come I was prone to volunteer the story of his death at dinner or cocktail parties, framed not as an emotional saga but as an up-tempo campfire shocker that somehow reflected well on the rest of us and how sturdy we were, how able we were to understand and accept the unhappy facts: *Hey! Check this out! I have a dead brother. Perfectly healthy guy, had just run a marathon the day before, then dropped dead, leaving behind a wife and three young children! Isn't that crazy?*

A few weeks after Todd died, our father organized a luncheon for the East Coast friends and family who hadn't flown west for the memorial. He had progressed from merely throwing impressive dinner parties at home to eventually owning, with my sister, a sixty-five-seat restaurant in our hometown, where the lunch was held. A few of us lingered awhile at the end—Melissa and Jeffrey and myself, my father's new wife, her daughter, a couple of old family friends—sitting at the long table out on the restaurant's patio, amid crumpled napkins and spent wineglasses, me now with an infant son in my arms. A family of ducks floated along on the slow-moving canal below. Someone sighed and mentioned it was sad that Todd himself couldn't have been here, at the gathering celebrating his own life, and there was a murmur of agreement all around, a pause, and then, as if to signal the end of the lunch and the beginning of our life as a diminished family, my dad said, "Well, if you have to lose one, at least it's the one you liked least."

I smiled reflexively at this, almost giggling like a child in church, and started to gather my bag and the Moses basket and head to my car. I imagine I had always known, but still, the bluntness was startling. I found myself thrilling uncomfortably, struck by this little doozy that he dropped on those of us who had remained in earshot at the table. *It could have been worse,* he seemed to be saying, gathering up the dirty napkins and brushing crumbs onto the gravel. It could have been one of his kids that he liked.

The ability to discern which of the deaths of your own children is the better death, to be able to pull one from the lineup and say, *Well, if one had to go, at least it was this one,* struck me in the moment as a mark of his exceptionalness. Most fathers, I would have thought, regular fathers, would have responded to the death of a son with rage or depression or denial, but here was our exceptional, nonconforming father instead throwing an al fresco lunch and remarking on his luck.

I had known, of course I had, that we were ranked. But on this particular day, hearing so baldly that he had "least liked" our freshly dead brother, I found myself disturbed by it and I started to have a niggling sense that I would like to keep my distance from this man going forward. With Marco clipped tight in the rear-facing car seat, I drove carefully back to New York.

IT RUNS IN THE FAMILY

E VEN WITH TODD DEAD, and those of us remaining in various internecine states of fraying mutual regard or thick and clotty discord, I couldn't have pointed to anything amiss in the family bloodstream.

Some people can describe the tragedies that occur in their families in shorthand:

> *a long history of mental illness*
> *a legacy of crippling addiction*
> *a family history of breast cancer that goes all the way*
> *   back*

These deaths can be organized and therefore understood—no matter how unbearable—with the comprehensible *It runs in the family.*

But the most serious afflictions I would have diagnosed in

our family around this time were crowded teeth and bushy eyebrows. I was certainly aware of an unsavory streak of hauteur, but I always felt that we compensated for it with a winning dose of self-deprecation and an unstinting work ethic. Even though I knew we were a family veined through with certain brutalities, rifts, and unresolved conflicts, as well as some remarkable violences and some decades-long silences, I thought of those black-and-blue marks as if they were the desirable spores of mold found in noble cheeses. As if they were marks of strong character, a colorfulness to be cultivated and celebrated, and I wasn't able to see us as anything other than a robust and charismatic tribe. The great insult in our family was "precious," per our father, or worse, "humorless," as decreed by our mother, and I refused to be labeled as either. I thought of us, with all of our funny little ways of going, as Particularly Capable. Admirably Scrappy. Enduring. Straight shooting.

Even when my father began to have ailments—diabetes and then prostate cancer and, later still, stents sewn into all four quadrants of his heart—he was throwing dinner parties at his home, cooking elaborate meals, collecting punch lines and one-liners, and still showing up at his restaurant, to "work the room." I didn't think of him as having poor health so much as having ailments as a consequence of his willful, legendary noncompliance.

He delighted in stopping at each table to schmooze with the guests, and he remained devoted to his tap dancing lessons even well into his eighties, in spite of having had one of his legs amputated. "My tempo's not great," he quipped, tableside, and the customers were charmed. So was I. He rarely did what the doctors told him to do and was never quite able to give up what he was asked to give up. He was willing, I suppose, to forfeit a leg for the enjoyment of his nonconformity. I wonder if we didn't all inherit a streak of this, too.

About his own upbringing, my father only spoke of how he had had the best of everything, and he did not convey any sense of disappointment in his own parents. The most damning thing he ever said about his mother was that she was a bit of a social climber, but he said this with a chuckle, as if he admired it. He was proud of his name, his hometown, and his place in it. And our mother had always reported the same about her own childhood experience. She was especially proud of her Frenchness, her cultured upbringing, her father's considerable musical career, and her mother's clever resourcefulness. Even though she rolled her eyes in amiable exasperation when occasionally describing her father as a "tightwad," she only ever described her own childhood as rich and full.

To believe the things we believe about our families, to be able to describe them each in our own way with some emphasis here and some omission there, is to be able to declare about ourselves the things we wish to be true. At the time it occurred, I took Todd's death not only as a freakish lightning-strike event, but also as a credential. As if it were tangible confirmation that We—We the Good-Humored, Hardworking, Sleeve-Rolling, Realistic, Truth-Confronting Hamiltons—are a sturdy people who know how to move along and are never floored. We are a family who finds everything funny. A family who can even make fun of the way we have of finding everything funny. We are a family who insists that simply going for a brisk walk will cure everything and who can matter-of-factly declare that there is a bright side to everything, including the death of your least-liked son. A family who can readily metabolize the matter-of-fact facts.

We never slack, or list, or run aground. Thank-you notes, kisses on both cheeks, phone etiquette, table manners, firm handshakes, champagne at Christmas, good posture, *You wash; I'll dry* team spirit, and a *suck it up* attitude toward our dreaded chores and our tedious responsibilities. That is what I could say about my family, and myself, at this time. There was not one thing I could possibly name as mortally concerning that "runs in the family."

Though my mother and I had been firmly estranged for fifteen years when Todd suddenly died, I picked up a pen and, for the first time, reached out to her; I sent her a condolence card. If anything runs in the family, it's good manners.

(Interlude)

HOUSEKEEPING

A BIT OF HOUSEKEEPING. For the fact-checkers, but also for those of us who wash our washing machines, who rinse the recycling before we recycle, who become agitated when we find the toilet paper roll is installed "backward."

Technically and factually, my mother's house at the top of the mountain does not sit on one hundred acres as I earlier claimed; she is now surrounded by only fifty-eight acres because she has had to sell some parcels over time to make ends meet. I know this not from doing research in public records but because technically and factually, our thirty-year estrangement proceeded in two consecutive, discrete fifteen-year segments, broken—or bridged, depending on your view—by one thirty-six-hour hiatus in between, and I learned about the sales then, in person. The first leg of our estrangement proceeded as I've described for exactly fifteen years and was interrupted only when my first brother died and then ten days later my first son was born. Upon Marco's birth it immediately occurred to me that I should arrange for him to have his own relationship with his grandmother, should he grow up to want that. So directly after sending her my condolences I found myself writing her a separate postcard proposing a visit to introduce her to her brand-new grandson. She wrote back enthusiastically, and consequently, I drove up to her house and spent an afternoon with her and my Italian husband and my infant to somehow signal that they were all welcome to know one another should that be rewarding for them. What my infant son could have understood from that thirty-six-hour interlude is nothing; but there are photos of him being held in the sunny garden room by his grandmother, and she commenced sending him birthday cards and Christmas greetings every year thereafter.

"You know, I always loved the little soft babies. Still *do*!" she leans down into the bassinet and declares. Putting a little fuzzy edge to her voice, she coos, "I see 'em in the grocery store and I just can't stop myself. The 'dorable l'il things! Irresistible!"

She rubs her nose against Marco's, bundled tight there in his cotton blanket, and jokes, "Loves kittens; hates cats," thus making a good-humored, self-aware dig at her own lifelong contradictions. And in so doing, also giving him—while still in swaddling cloths, the way some mothers play Mozart tapes to their babies in utero—an early introduction to one of her core values: Everything Should Be Found Amusing.

But when I drove away after thirty-six hours I knew I would not pursue further rapprochement. I had found her, after all these years apart, neither too controlling nor too unbearable,

not even suffocating. Something else occurred; I found myself
Totally Bored. She had, remarkably, not changed in any way
since last I knew her. Her socks and her eye pencil and her
cooking spoons and her self-aware quips, the very same ones.
She seemed to me like a docent in a museum of herself—and
she walked you chirpily through the halls of her own dust-
covered portraits, the tour she had already been giving for decade upon decade. I felt oddly fixated on and repelled by her
knee socks, the very same actual physical socks I had last seen
her in, mended repeatedly; at the time of this visit she had
taken to using rubber bands to hold them up as the elastics
had long ago worn out.

"And here, Gabri, are the archives I keep of all the family
members, photos and news clippings and letters received and
so on. Oh, how I love written correspondence!"

"And this is the radio station I listen to—classical, *natch*,
given my upbringing."

"And this is what I cooked for lunch yesterday; I find a little
salade composée just right still, yes."

"And in fact I do go to bed around seven o'clock, as it gets
dark so early here behind the mountain in the winter."

She finds herself—and all of her mannerisms and her
habits—rather pleasing. She is self-charmed. To me, nothing
could be deadlier.

And I understood starkly that what I was leaving behind
up on that hilltop, receding in the rearview mirror—she there
in her house, with her fixed routines and her steadfast prefer-
ences and her undisturbed solitude, her same witty quips, her
salads for dinner and her 7:00 P.M. bedtime—was something
of a mausoleum. One with streaming sunlight and expansive
views of the surrounding hills and fresh sylvan breezes, but

still, one with all of its contents—her dinner napkins and her butter knives and her push-button telephone and even her opinions and emotions and appetites—congealed as if in a stiff wax. And you, You, remote, looking down from outside of your own body, realized that it would all be just exactly where you left it no matter how many decades might pass, no matter what magnitude of life's buffeting experiences may rip the weathervanes off our family's lives; you saw that she would be there, exactly there, uncannily embalmed in her own self-satisfaction. You held the bundle of your newborn fast in your arms and bent to kiss your mother goodbye without allowing her body to touch yours. And in the car, you yawned incessantly during the long drive back to New York. So, you didn't need to return. You had made the right decision for yourself long ago and there was nothing to regret; you had not missed out on anything.

And neither had she. She was not laid low by the loss of you. By your absence. By missing out on who you had become—for better and for worse—in the intervening years. She had photos of a long-ago you pinned to her bulletin board above her desk, and she liked looking at the you she had captured—and stilled—there. She was not evidently diminished by the loss of Todd, either. For whom, incidentally, I could never find a corroborating record of his alleged Mensa membership in her archive—fact-checker beware! But there was his youthful photo under a magnet on the refrigerator door. His collected postcards in a stack on her desk. Her daily coo-coo'ing hello to him as she reaches for the half-and-half.

Naïvely, prone to bouts of sentimentality since giving birth, I had been expecting to see something of a mark left on her by these losses, some shadow, a dimness in her light. But she appeared unharmed and exuberant and buoyant. Her sense of humor robust as ever. I don't know how long a mother has to carry around the markers of her unspeakable grief at having lost a child, at what month or year she is allowed to shed some of that uncarryable weight, but I would have thought that at just these few months since he'd died that there would have been more lingering evidence of it. In its absence, I wondered if by moving herself to Vermont those decades ago she had secured for herself what she most cherished—solitude, freedom, distance—days and days and a lifetime of days without being disturbed or encumbered by the requirements and the particularities of her children.

There is still a dullness in my own mind, I haven't miraculously outgrown it, but at last it clears for a lucid moment, and I see that it is only me who is hoping to be missed, to be longed for, to have my absence be found intolerable. It is only me who wants the death of our brother to have left a crater in our parents' lives. Not that they should suffer but that we might know that we have mattered. I will look ahead in my own parenting life to say often that if my own kids ever didn't talk to me for fifteen years, or complained of chronic headaches and sleepless nights, or called for help, or presented challenges more challenging than a chewable aspirin could solve, I would drive across the whole country no matter how many miles, and I would find their houses, walk up all the flights of stairs to their apartments, get down on my stomach on the welcome mat, and cry into the crack under the door—*I am here to see you. I am here to see you.*

Waving gently from the car as I pull out of her driveway, I am already thinking like this. As if I am still getting started and I am still on my way somewhere, with a new baby in the back seat—and as if I will do it all differently, as if I will cherry-pick only our parents' admirable traits and handily distance myself and my children from their less admirable ones. As if I will do it all the right way and make a robust family of my own and tend to it for its lifetime. So, I let her go, again. And this time, for keeps. Or so I think.

Part Three

PROFESSIONALS DELIVER

I'M DOUBLE-PARKED OUTSIDE my restaurant, waiting
for the street sweeper to pass, when my father calls. He
wants to congratulate me.

My restaurant has just had a review in *The New York
Times,* and it's positive.

When I answer the phone, he greets me with a strangled
"Heeeyyy?" that is wan and questioning, where it should be
saturated and declarative.

"Gah-beez."

"Hey, Dad," I say, both alert and resigned, like when you
find yourself in the clinic chair, arm strapped, about to have
blood drawn.

Then he offers a slow, drawn-out "con . . . graddddd—
yewwww-lay-shunnnns" as if he's reading out of a Berlitz
phrase book. I hasten him along. He has explicitly wanted *The*

New York Times to recognize his own restaurant ever since he opened it, and they have not done so.

"Thanks, Dad, it's really nothing. How's it going with *you*?"

He has a new joke he's been fond of lately, that he wants to drop on me:

"Who sleeps with Katz?"

"I don't know, Dad. Who sleeps with cats?"

"Mrs. Katz!"

I chuckle genuinely. "Oh, Dad. Okay. Okay."

Our conversations are one-sided and bright and easygoing, focused on him and his news, but if there is ever something in the paper about me or written by me, I brace myself for his eventual call, which always reminds me of one of those frustrating overseas calls with delay and echo and cross-talk, because he doesn't excel at what to do when it's about you and not him, and I try to get them over with quickly. My father reads *The New York Times* every day. Each morning, he starts with the obituaries, his favorite section; goes deep on some of the front page; skitters through business and finance; inhales city, arts and leisure; glances at sports; tears out the food section to cook from later; then leaves the crossword puzzle for bedtime. He has obviously not missed the positive review.

"Well," he says, and then there's a pause. He's setting up a humorous bit, I hear it in the purposeful stall, the gentle clearing of his throat. "I've had a sign made out here, because I get asked all the time about you by *all your adoring fans . . .*" He goes heavy on the sarcasm here, before he gets to his punch line. "It says, 'Gabrielle's Father,' and I hang it at the restaurant whenever there's something in the paper about you."

"Oh, poor you," I say, chuckling. "I'm sorry."

His is a funny mix; he's proud of my successes, I have to imagine, because surely they reflect well on him, and he respects quality work, I am certain. But he also fears and loathes being eclipsed. He and I are in the regular position lately of receiving each other's admirers. The servers in my restaurant will sometimes pop into the kitchen and ask me to stop by table 9 on the banquette, or table 1 in the corner, or 4 in the window—to say hello to someone they're waiting on. *It's a friend of your father's,* they tell me. I set bright eyes and a strong smile.

Hello! So nice to meet you! You know my dad?

I give my best tableside schmooze.

What brings you into the city? Oh yes, that Matthew Barney thing was wild, yes. Oh, how was Print? *I've been meaning to see that but haven't gotten to it yet.*

But we both know what she really wants to talk about.

Oh my goodness, your father. Oh, your father!

She takes a sip of her red wine.

A genius!

Your dad

designed our kitchen

designed our house

cooked for my daughter's wedding

invited us to dinner at his home

designed our addition on our house

cooked for us at his restaurant

helped us renovate an old barn on our property

cooked at an auction we bid on

helped our son get a job at a restaurant in Philly

cooked for our son's engagement party!

"He's a good one, he really is," I say, nodding in agreement.

I have no idea what he has had to receive on his end, in re-turn, but I know many of our regulars get out to his restau-rant. And the people who read my articles, too. The corridor between our hometown and New York City is pretty direct—ninety minutes on Route 78, sixty-five minutes on Amtrak. Whoever they are, he makes it sound as if they are a nuisance, and grossly misguided. He has had to put up with *all my ador-ing fans,* evidently.

"Nah, it's exciting, Gabs, come on," he says. "It'll be good for your business. Congratulations."

"Thanks, Dad. Thanks for calling," I say, taking advantage of what seems to be a natural point to end the call. I can hear the street sweeper honking its way down the block, its brushes furiously spinning. I want to ease back into my parking spot as soon as it passes.

But he's not finished.

"You know what I don't get, though, Gabs, is that there's so much equal or greater talent out there, how did they decide it was your turn, you know?"

"I know, Dad. Right? Why me? It's crazy and hard to un-derstand. I agree. I'm not quite sure, honestly."

It has been a lifetime of him by now, and we, all of his chil-dren, have sprouted up around him, like energetic saplings that twist themselves right around an abutting section of barbed wire fencing or telephone line or pasture posting where it has become fixed into our trunks as we pushed upward to the sunlight. We have all made accommodations for him, not all of them wholesome. Contorting and giggling and over-achieving and underachieving and redirecting focus and mir-roring and emulating and arriving at parties with already opened bottles of wine. You cannot suppress your own sapling nature—of course you are driven, you strive for the goldest of golden pears to hang heavy and ripe from your own branches—but you know to be careful as you shoot up and try not to cast any shadow. Curiously, none of us has ever fully cut him loose, slammed down the phone, walked away, or declared him more trouble than he's worth. I've kept him at a friendly, effective distance—he has met my husband once, eaten at my restaurant twice, and he has met my still-young children a few times in passing—as he prefers. "Don't bother me with the little ones who can't even do anything yet; I only start to like 'em when they're old enough to ski!" he declares when each is born, and we laugh about this. *Oh, Dad.*

But somehow—in this moment, on this day, this particular candor about my equal or lesser talent—strikes me somehow as belligerent, and I feel a long-dormant imperative to put an end to it. Maybe it's the sixteen-hour restaurant days, the two young children, the thirty employees, the side-hustle writing deadlines, the chore of parking the stupid car: I don't feel like being a good sport. But instead of letting him know I will never speak to him again and hanging up the phone, I find myself with the urge to rescue us both, to fix the problem of his bad habits. I have been enthralled by this man since I met him. He's special. Talented. Funny. Charming. Hardworking. Large-hearted. Interesting. If he could just be talked out of his compulsion to crush underfoot his own talented children, he'd be perfect. And in this otherwise mundane moment of New York City alternate-side parking and street sweeping, with my dad insulting me when he should be congratulating me, I find myself simply wanting what I want. It's a distinctly clean and dry and gentle feeling of freedom, to be this tired of his bullshit.

"Um, Dad, you know, I don't know if it matters to you, but you're going to die at some point sooner than later, and I'm starting to think I'm only going to be able to remember you in this way, if you don't stop it. I now have more experiences of you saying shit like this about all of us kids than I have good experiences of you, and so, in case it matters to you, this is how I'm probably going to remember you, always with these put-downs."

I was proud of my tone, my defanged and matter-of-fact observation when I told him about what it was doing to me, to us. I was not cornering him, or scolding him, as I had as a seventeen-year-old; I was leaving him plenty of room.

He was startled. Cleared his throat, as he does. "Huh. Gabs. I didn't know! I just thought that's what we did in this family. I just don't want your head to get too swollen."

To which I laughed out loud and reassured him his work was done; he really needn't worry.

And he said, "Well, I'll be more careful, Gabs, now that I know."

"K, Dad. Thanks," I say.

I park the car and go to work. There are a ton of messages waiting for me, the kind regular people offer when something good happens, congratulatory, well-wishing, all caps and lots of exclamation points and encouragement. WAY TO GO! WELL-DESERVED! NICE WORK, LADY!

But you, You, you apologize, weirdly, shrug your thanks, and you giggle your undeservingness.

꘠

WHEN YOU ARE a kid one early summer day, you accidentally roll the sit-down mower by taking a little hillock in the
back meadow too fast—you come running home to your dad,
shaken, trembling, you've leapt from the runaway machine
just in time to avoid being crushed by it, and while you are trying to blame the hillock, or the mower, or the slippery grass,
he shrugs: "Professionals deliver. Amateurs explain. Do you
want to be known as a person who doesn't finish the job?"
There was no *I'm only a kid, the machine is too powerful, the
dog ate my homework, the boss is a bitch, the pay is insulting,
the field is dominated by men* in his book of Professionalism.
That was what amateurs said; they made excuses and had
lengthy explanations. He went and got the mower upright,
checked the gas and oil, and put you, shaking, back on it.
"Professionals deliver."

But to deliver, it turns out—to yield golden pears—is its
own peculiar hazard. You have done everything exactly as you
have been shown. You have listened intently, observed carefully, absorbed capaciously, understood what was required,
and delivered. You are discerning, colorful, hardworking, and
humorous. You never advertise any of your honorable mentions or nominations or even your wins; you earn all of your
own money and are never a burden on anyone in any way, you
are nonconforming, bohemian, thick-skinned, a servant to
"the good story," a professional who delivers, who can take a
joke, who is always a good sport. You have listened to every
word of the homily, and devoutly tithed, as it were, to his
church. Nonetheless, he will forever want to discuss with you
your equal or lesser talents and to wonder out loud with you
how it got to be your turn.

THE BURNING SHIP

T HERE IS A cherished annual summer vacation. August in
Italy, every year, when my sons are still very young, and I
am still married to their Italian father. We always spend a few
days in Rome at the family apartment, but the real vacation
starts when we finally head south, to spend the month in Pu-
glia, where the fennel grows wild, and where we remain barefoot the whole time except to walk into town for il giornale
and a few breakfast cornetti. One morning a large boat catches
fire while anchored in the bay in front of the family house in
Leuca. The boat's steward had left laundry running in the
dryer while they went ashore for restocking and provisioning.
No one had remained behind, so no one needed to be rescued,
no crew member needed to call below to the cooks, "Abandon
ship! Abandon ship!" The Vigili del Fuoco Marittimi arrived
eventually, but, instead of opening their hoses and attempting
the struggle to put the fire out, they decided to let it burn.

It takes a long time for a boat to burn itself to death. It burned throughout the day and into the night for days on end, rescue and fire boats formed a ring around it, and meanwhile marina life bustled on as usual. Swordfishing boats departed in the night and returned with the sunrise. Private colossal Russian yachts—like floating discotheques with red and blue pulsing lights and technotronic music—continued their sea-bound parties undeterred, and all the while this boat burned in the harbor.

We would come out on the terrace with our coffee in the mornings and watch its progress before heading back in for breakfast, for a day with the kids at the swimming pool, for siesta, and then again, checking from the terrace before dinner with a Negroni, and again after dinner. That burning boat somehow hung there for days, afloat but dead from the waist down, as one vital piece and then another, one by one—a fuse box, a water pump, a winch motor—burned out, each element in its own time, while flames roared skyward from the boat's torso. An incomprehensible spectacle of burning water. When we woke finally to a flat line of horizon, it was over.

I'd all along been actively reflective, analytical, critical even, about my own upbringing, my family's character, my inherited values—but even that summer, when I am well into my forties, I am still convinced of the charms of "complicat-edness," and bohemia, and contrarian ways of going, and still proud of our unorthodoxies and dark humor. This summer when the boat is burning in front of the house, I am not yet divorced but neither am I very married. I've carelessly em-barked on a marriage that was never seaworthy to begin with, never meant for the journey it would be asked to make, and even though I know this, I am not willing to concede to it, because I am determined to have a family that lasts. Years from now I will meet and work with an analyst who says, in short, *I believe people know exactly everything about themselves within minutes of knowing it, but they then spend an unbelievable amount of time dicking around with the inconvenient information.* But I haven't met him yet. So, I am still in the habit of expending terrific energy *dicking around with the inconvenient information* instead of divorcing; I've made the bed a hundred different ways in order to be able to lie in it, and rather than admit the marriage's failure, I tout its nonconformity. The current iteration: We live separately in our own apartments in New York and shuttle the kids back and forth— he's uptown, I'm downtown—but for this one month each summer when we pile in with my husband's family in Italy. It is nothing short of breathtaking, how long I can coast on the fumes of this beloved annual vacation, breezily tucked in with his large and affectionate and entertaining family, to carry me through the other remaining bereft, and often volatile, eleven months of so-called marriage each year.

Naturally, I find myself hugely affronted by the Vigili del Fuoco, the way they lazily circle up, smoking cigarettes, wearing their dark aviator sunglasses, idling the throttles on their engines, and watching the spectacle of the burning boat, shrugging, determining that it is easier to let it go than to struggle to salvage it, until the whole thing has slipped, finally, under the water line and disappeared.

ON THE PARENTING FRONT, while I am not nearly as violent as my own mother, I have yanked many a hairbrush unsparingly through the knots and tangles of my boys' hair on late, agitated mornings getting to school. I have kicked the shit out of a kitchen garbage can, stunning the boys, if not terrifying them, during a kiddie dinner that was so unruly I felt I would explode. I don't ever share with them any of my financial worries, but I never use baby talk, never tailor my vocabulary to their ages, and speak to them as if they are adults. I have roared in a fit of pique about some behavior of theirs, demanding to know why they have had to act like "such cunts." The way my mother loved to introduce herself at dinner parties, as a young woman of her era enthralled with Dorothy Parker, was to quip, "If you haven't got anything nice to say about anybody, come sit next to me!"—and she delighted herself every time. At my own dinner parties, I laugh and joke, "I think it's important that children experience a little trauma; it's good for them!" and I delight myself with this little bit of cheekiness.

I see third-grade Leone double- and triple-checking the custody schedule repeatedly in his head before saying goodbye. The two-day-on-two-day-off rhythm of our arrangement, organized around our "alternative" marriage model, long since held fast in his still small body. "So, today is Monday," he says with his hand on the door, pausing before exiting the car, lingering in our last minute of custody, "then Tuesday, okay, so back on Wednesday! Bye!" and out the door—to school, to the doorman, to the apartment lobby. And I feebly hope that what the experts say is true: *Kids are resilient.*

I have pendulum-swung away from my own mother's mothering on just a few things—instead of always No, with me it is always Yes, which creates its own havoc, I will eventually recognize. But until I finally catch on, I will, for too many and for too crucial years, be a mother downstairs in her home kitchen who is incapable of calling her children to the dinner table at a set hour, a mother incapable of asking them to load a dishwasher. To walk a dog. To come say hello to the new neighbors. To eat the complex dinner she has cooked. To go on a bike ride. To endure their hostilities and grumbling unhappiness and exaggerated discomfort when I hazard even a tiny No. And instead of eye-rolling and dismissing out of hand everything they say about themselves, I swing defiantly to the opposite pole and make certain to honor and respect every attempt they make at self-defining along the way. Another minefield in its own way, navigable surely, through some middle path. But to do this, you have to have caught on to yourself and your rancid dark-blue molds, and I haven't yet.

I have an argument with fourth-grade Marco, and I allow it to become a horrible one, so that it runs off the rails, as if there were no adult in the room who might shepherd the outcome of things; instead, I accept every inflammatory invitation to spar. How does it end? He levels me with a blisteringly accurate, quietly delivered "It would be great if my mother didn't have the emotional maturity of a ten-year-old!" and asks to live with his father full-time.

But I have not picked up on even the tiniest glimmer of these things to come—that my sons will loathe me, that I am soon to be divorced, that my oldest brother is soon to kill himself, that my own father is going to declare me dead to him, that my sister is soon to be heard threatening to post a cop at the door of our father's memorial service if I dare to show up—and out on that terrace I stand, this unwitting last summer as a family together in Italy, with my young children, watching that boat burn, still convinced that the family I am stewarding is a righteous improvement on the one I came from, and that we, by force of my will, are going to make our full journey intact.

THE FRUIT DESCRIBES
THE TREE

B Y THE TIME Jeffrey killed himself, we were already dead
at sea, all of us, lost to each other with no chance of return.
It had generally been me who'd done the distancing, the door-
closing, the deciding. Me who'd put the phone down and
thought, *Cut it off. Cut it loose, or you'll never make it.* Always
calmly, definitively, and—of particular note—nonviolently. Without quarrel or combustion. But then, out of nowhere, without a
hint it was lurking in me, I found myself taping a bundle of dy-
namite to the trestle of my last bridge to home, to family, to be-
longing, and blowing it up. My own sister's husband and I
became a couple, after their twenty-three years of marriage.

Technically and factually, we'd become a couple *again*.
We'd agonized over it scrupulously, an impossible word to use
for a decision that exhibits no scruples, but then, tremblingly,
we became again something we'd been twenty-four years earlier, before he married my sister. Boyfriend and girlfriend.

I was vehemently against the idea, against even mentioning the idea, against the breathing, even, of such an idea. We'd been Family with a capital F for capital F Forever. For decades already he'd been the capable, very nice guy married to my sister, working for my father—who, for me, had an annoying streak of eternal boyishness he seemed to refuse to outgrow. He'd been, for over twenty years already, the guy there in the background behind my sister, thankfully *her problem, not mine*. When my boys and I would arrive for a weekend visit, he'd go upstairs and pull out the blow-up mattress from a remote closet, while my adored sister and I stayed down in the kitchen having martinis and cooking dinner and rattling away in nonstop chatter, finishing each other's sentences, nodding in constant agreement, howling at each other's funny quips. He'd put my boys in the back of the tractor mower and cart them around while doing outdoor chores, so Melissa and I could drink coffee with half-and-half and talk and talk and talk our brains out. He'd been my regular go-to for man-around-the-house questions: "Wait, Michael, if I'm putting sixteen chairs at this table, how many inches between table settings do I need to accommodate the chairs when people are seated, please?" He'd been the guy who did their daughters' school drop-offs and pickups each day; the "wheeler" who took a thirty-mile ride on his road bike almost every afternoon when he needed a work break; who was a trustee, then vice president, then treasurer of the historical mill society; who ran for borough council and won and remained the president for ten years; who got the cover off the swimming pool each year and adjusted the chlorine so that nobody's eyes stung; who had been a Cub Scout, a Boy Scout, a star scout, an altar boy; the one who always kept his pager on, then later his phone ringer, and who never missed the occasional calls from the school nurse or the camp counselors; who did all the demo work and the new electrical and the sheetrocking in their old house; who had perfected his from-scratch thin-crust dough with perfect char for pizza nights when the house was full of kids and Meliss was stuck on a non-negotiable work deadline, unable to be home until very late. The background figure who knew how to perform the Heimlich maneuver, to sail a sailboat, fix an exhaust manifold or a manual transmission, and use a Shop-Vac as a sump pump if the basement flooded. A massive Kurt Vonnegut fan with a soft spot for the Pittsburgh Steelers, who also had a habit of making uncomfortable personal decisions—a DUI in his twenties, a porn habit at the local video store, an insistence on referring to any woman he disliked as "a total gash," a profound social anxiety when meeting anyone new that he blustered his way through by shutting his eyes closed tight for long minutes, even while shaking their hand and loudly talking talking talking right over them like a verbal bulldozer. Our father often bluntly and publicly disparaged him as "uncreative" for the thirteen years Michael worked for him as a draftsman. If anyone ever praised Michael, our dad would raise his eyebrows noncommittally and say, "Is that so?" and then go on, explaining matter-of-factly that the real talent in that household was up front, residing in Melissa, my beloved sister. I generally agreed. I was all about Meliss.

For twenty-three years, Michael remained a steady, reliable, dependable background fixture of our family, like a lieutenant, or the drummer who keeps the band on tempo but never takes the mic, who helps when asked, who was loyal to his own parents, and dutiful with ours, who built the fires, put up the Christmas trees, lent money to Jeffrey when his truck broke down, and who shone exceedingly brightly in just one regard, as far as I was concerned—the exceptional exception—in his colossal talent as Uncle Michael. Oh, how he loved my boys. And, oh, how my boys loved him. The wood-whittling and creek-walking and tractor-mowing and football-throwing and the tire swing rides and soft-serve ice cream and french fries and grilled cheeses and the pirate bandannas and the swimming pool games of "jump or dive," the rock, paper, scissors and the gin rummy using the coin jar as ante and the trampolining on the couch and the leaf-raking piles. Uncle. Michael.

But after twenty-three years of being brother-in-law, of being *Uncle Michael,* he had left me a message: *I need to talk to you. I'm fucked up.* And the second I took in those words, I realized what he was going to reveal. After two days of ignoring it, I shot back: *Under no circumstances will we ever have this conversation.*

IN THE SUMMER of that year, just a couple of months before that fateful text, I'd retreated out to their house for a short getaway with my boys. My own divorce finally in motion, with the usual decamping to Italy scraped off the table and dropped in the trash, I'd reached out to my sister. "Any chance I can invite myself over for a few days? Any room at the inn?" I'd asked. Melissa had warned that she'd be buried at work the whole week on a massive deadline, but she encouraged me to come out anyway and to take advantage of the pool and the

fresh country air and the path along the canal to practice riding bikes with my boys instead of staying cooped up in the
tiny apartment in New York. And for that week I tried to com-
pensate for being an uninvited houseguest with two rowdy
children by acting as a kind of jolly placeholder for her, like a
well-rested understudy stepping in while the lead who has
been carrying eight shows a week is out on family emergency.
I cooked the dinners and made the martinis and did the household's laundry and had long, thoughtful auntie conversations
with my nieces, who were—*holy shit!*—both heading out to
their colleges in just a few weeks, and then I had long contem-
plative conversations with Michael, who was heavy-hearted
and acutely lamenting the empty nest upon the near horizon.

As we were pulling out of the driveway at the end of the
week to head back to New York, Michael quickly popped his
head into the back seat to kiss the boys goodbye one more
time, and I saw that he was crying. And I laughed to the boys
out loud in the rearview mirror, "Oh my god, boys, check it
out! Uncle Michael is having separation anxiety, I do believe!"
and I chuckled at the open display of sentiment in front of us,
smiling at Michael the same way you might pet a dog's head.
Oh, you little dear softie. It had been a great visit, easygoing
and familial. We made jokes to Melissa, when she dragged herself home well after midnight, that I was the perfect surrogate
wife and he my ideal stand-in husband, and that we should
have arranged it like this long, long ago! We all laughed. I reported back to Melissa during one of our zillion phone calls,
"I actually kind of love Michael, now, Meliss. Don't you? I
mean, I think he's really growing and maturing. No?" I felt
tender admiration for a grieving brother-in-law who adored

his daughters beyond beyond beyond, who was on the sad cusp of living in an empty house and who was open-heartedly soul-searching over it.

"Goodbye, Uncle Michael!!!!" the boys sang out to him and waved and blew kisses as we rolled out of the driveway and drove back to the city.

That message, then, out of the blue, unlike any we had exchanged before, startled me. Twenty-three years of questions about tiling grout or paint chips or standard counter height or the right butterfly anchors for mounting a heavy wall cabinet, and suddenly he was here saying, *I need to talk to you. I'm fucked up.*

BACK WHEN WE were in our twenties, when he was *just my boyfriend*—a way of phrasing it so that taxonomies of wounding or transgression can be established—he and my sister had an affair. We had all eventually been sturdy and practical about it. We made jokes, even—"Right family, wrong sister, whoops!" A fuckup like that in your youth is one thing. Even though we were a We, Michael and I, I had been suspicious of his steady niceness, accused him of being an enabler, a codependent type, and I was not imagining sticking around for long. Living in my father's basement apartment, saving money, poring over atlases and Lonely Planet guidebooks, I had already been, for months, dreaming up a long solo trip abroad. We knew that we would not be a We forever. But the shock and sting of their affair was the final impetus to hastily gather my passport, Imodium tablets, and a quinine prescription and leave the country right away. In evacuating the scene immediately, I afforded them a bit of privacy in which to rearrange the details of their beginnings without the public evidence and the generally squirmy discomfort we would have felt if I had remained in plain sight. Without me smoldering in the background as an inconvenient piece of data, it would become easier to edit and shape their origin story; to resort to the technical and factual "he was working for my father at the time . . ." Otherwise, whenever the new couple was asked casually, "Oh, how did you two get together?" the truer story would have carried with it a whiff of shame. We joked about it openly among the three of us years later. "Revisionist History! That's right, baby!" we quipped, howling with laughter.

But still, even though it had been gently omitted from their origin story, I always suspected that the affair must've remained somewhere in the marriage, embedded in the framework like one of those load-bearing cast iron vertical beams in a renovated loft that frustrates your design dreams and cannot safely or structurally be removed.

As I checked in and out of freezing-cold youth hostels in the dead of winter, I worked overtime, with ardor, to get right with their betrayal, to brush it off, to save face, to find a way to remain a head-held-high member of my lively, colorful, unique, special, somewhat treacherous family. How many notebooks, in how many cafés, did I fill with my bleak heart's contents? I am embarrassed to count. But after a couple of years of this, I agreed to accept my sister's shrugging matter-of-factness when she finally wrote me a letter, breaking her silence, and announcing their decision to marry. "This kind of thing happens all the time, Gabs. The only thing that's weird about it is that we're sisters. Honestly, I don't think anyone here even thinks about it anymore. You don't have to worry about coming home."

When their affair took that turn toward marriage—according to the taxonomy: a real and substantial arrangement—I understood that I had better get my feelings thoroughly worked out.

I wanted everyone to be free and happy, I wanted to be able to finally come home after two years of backpacking and youth hosteling around the globe, and I wanted my return to be welcomed, not dreaded.

When I returned, I devoted myself to finally finishing my last semester of college, to getting myself settled thereafter in New York, and to making the whole hometown situation ostentatiously, publicly, formally condoned. Melissa and I had been more or less collegial and sisterly up until the affair, but never superlative or emphatic or gushy about each other. *Now is our time,* I decide. I don't know how I decide this, but it ties into some ideas I am starting to have about myself, about Feminism and being on the side of women, about my Platonic Aesthetics, my own expression of Form and Beauty. There are heroes of mine at that age—I love romantic yet stoic, cool but passionate. Mostly literary figures—I model myself after Anne Sexton, Lillian Hellman, Ernest Hemingway, Lawrence Durrell, Somerset Maugham, a bit of Colette, a larger bit of Henry Miller. I like my heroes masculine or at least mannish. The women I admire smoke cigarettes, keep up drink for drink with the men, and keep their writing tight. Muscular. And their emotions known, but controlled.

But it's confusing as I'm also very attracted to the hunger strikers. And the monks who set themselves on fire for their political convictions. People who chain themselves to the desks at huge pharmaceutical companies to demand effective afford-able drugs for AIDS patients. It's a brew. A mix. A classic twenty-year-old's grab bag of personas and philosophies and ideas. Also, I feel a little sorry for my sister; I would never marry someone with whom I'd had an affair, because they have already revealed their character.

Whenever I visit, I go around our hometown as if I am the matchmaker who has set this whole thing up; I make myself indispensable in their union. I persuade people who might be otherwise scandalized not to be. *It happens, man,* I say. I seek literary precedent—who in the canon has experienced betrayal before me and how they handled it. Would I, Medea-like, exact devastating revenge on my unfaithful Jason? *Too emotional. Too hysterical,* I decide. I prefer the type of protagonist who takes a long drag on her cigarette and surveys the perplexing scene in front of her as she discovers the affair—my sister is arriving home very early in the morning and my boyfriend is driving the car, the top is down, the birdsong has only just begun as it is near dawn, and I, I happen to have pulled an all-nighter writing in my basement apartment at the top of the hill and I happen to look out the window and register what is happening in my own driveway, as they duck down to kiss goodbye—and I decide to see myself as a type of cinematic figure, the type of woman I've seen in foreign films, a woman who can exhale coolly: *It's for the best.*

I DECIDE I am Family. I prefer it to the embarrassing sting of Cuckold. Of "also-ran." I position myself in my mind as the one who has cast him off, her as the one who agreed to "sloppy seconds," and us all as "everything works out in the end, after all, as it is meant to."

I make a show of my new attitude, and I laugh and cheer at their wedding party in case anyone is looking at me out of the side of their eye. Our father tinkles his glass and misquotes Pablo Casals, and I tear up. I help build the new crib and throw the baby shower for the arriving first child. I marriage counsel when that child brings the usual frictions and tensions into the home. Melissa's joke at the time is "Children: They're what drives you apart, and what forces you to have to stay together." And she laughs her lively soprano-flute laugh, punching in on a high note and dropping to the lowest register on its staccato descent. I side with her unequivocally during any tension between them, declare my fidelity not only to my sister but to their healthy marriage. I say, *This has already cost a lot, this situation, so let's not blow it.* But I also always let Michael know that I empathize with anyone who has to deal with a Hamilton. I claim him as a full brother—not just an in-law, but a legitimate sixth sibling. You will never know an empath as empathic as myself. I'm not aware of any of this. And no one is stopping me. No one is saying, *Thanks but no thanks.* I imagine everyone is just massively grateful and relieved that I am making it so easy for them, and that I am not making a scene. I take pride in this.

LIKE ANY SELF-RESPECTING New Yorker, I get a shrink. Everyone I meet has one, talks about it as casually as if they had gotten a MetroCard, and seems not to be shouldering even one smoldering remnant of the queasy embarrassment they would have carried if they'd stayed in their own provincial hometowns and been found out as the humorless, oversensitive "pussy" in their own family who has had to pay somebody to listen to their supposed problems. At that time, I'm in the tiny offices of very nice ladies all in the vicinity of University Place whose eyebrows rise up and arc in compassionate seagull wings when I talk. Reliably, each one I engage over the following decades makes her care and warmth palpable in the room, and it's nice, and I like going. But I am suspicious of Nice. Nice makes me squirm. Even though I am aware on some level that it's not supposed to. At some point I try group therapy, too, thinking that with many other people in the room there will be a welcome distraction of the arched concerned eyebrows that in individual counseling are always only focused on you. I can't bear to be babied. Or attended to. Or cared about. When I later finish grad school and start living with a cherished soulmate girlfriend of several years, I get us to go to couples therapy, too, to see what that's all about. Individual, group, couples—I go almost athletically, and I will come to judge anyone who doesn't, or who only goes in crisis. I scold anyone who stops going a few sessions later when they feel better having let off some steam. "You can't use it like that!" I admonish. "It's a long game, like going to the gym or to language class," I say. "You can't get buff or fluent if you only go a few sessions and then quit once you learn a few phrases!" As if I think I am Socrates himself, at Delphi, guarding the marble where it is etched, KNOW THYSELF.

But some decades later I had graduated—not everyone sees it that way—to analysis, farther uptown, in the Flatiron. Three days a week on the couch, lying down, analyst behind me, no

eye contact, or arched eyebrows, or any other exhausting social signals passing between us. At every session I throw up
onto the blank wall whatever's on my mind, like a human pro-
jector, and, together, we "read" the footage. He happens to be
an expert, my analyst, a phenomenal reader in the British Re-
lational School who picks up on tropes and verbal tics and
narrative arcs and subtext and supertexts and unreliable source
material and giggling as nervous deflection—"What's with all
the giggling," he asks, "when the material is hardly funny?"
He also gently but audibly sighs from his chair behind me
when he wishes to signal to me that I have exhausted his formidable talents. He refuses to be referred to as "my shrink" and
bristles at the term: "I've never shrunk anything in my life; I
try to expand," he points out.

While my family will outwardly argue, in keeping with
our strong streak of noblesse oblige, that obviously people
sometimes need help, inwardly we are proudly certain that
we, ourselves, would never. We will be the ones to graciously
provide, not to brokenly receive. We find it a little inferior, a
little self-indulgent when people can't just get their shit together on their own, like quitting smoking the only respectable way: cold turkey. And Jeffrey, by nature, is vocal about it.
"Whoa, Gabs, really? Therapy? Analysis? What's so baaaad
that you have to talk it all out?" We are standing in the
kitchen at Melissa and Michael's house one morning; he is
nursing a minor hangover by toking hard on his one-hitter to
go with his coffee as he tries to get his day started. He draws
out the word "bad" and wiggles his head from side to side,
stiffly holding up both hands to mock my implied *boo-hoo-
hoo* self-involvement. "I'm just saying, I mean, sorry, Gabs,
but you must be really fucked up." And here he cracks him-

self up, choking a little on his hashish exhale, letting out that
lion's roar of his.

FOR THE DURATION of their twenty-three years of marriage, I will always drive out from New York to help with celebration meals, with restaurant shifts, with housesitting and
lawn mowing, will always keep the sheets clean and ready on
the pullout couch in my own apartment, available for Meliss
whenever she comes into the city for work and needs a place to
spend the night. And she will become the sole member of my
family who will always "get" me, who will consistently behave
properly, righteously, unconditionally; she welcomes my visits,
loves my work, supports my decisions, praises my character,
admires my talents, unstintingly celebrates my successes.

It's easy to deride the twenty-year-old self, long ago standing
there looking out the window trying to decipher the confusing
and painful scene, immediately and reflexively auditioning literary characters to play her role in the drama unspooling in
front of her eyes. *Who can I be right now who is not stupid
me, who will do a much more dignified job than regular, petty,
burning-hot me?* Yet I don't. I hold that person dear. Her
searchingness. Her convictions. Her resolve to play it cool,
sober, and offhand when she felt nuclear. I wish I could have
maintained her ethic.

BUT THAT REVERSE tipping of the seesaw decades later, in
my late forties—now her husband was again my boyfriend—

this was something else altogether, no matter the explanations or the circumstances. Michael and I somehow decided to go forth with something impossible to justify, and we couldn't work our way out of it.

I said, *Over my dead body. We will never discuss this.*

And he said, *I believe, then, you are going to have to be dead to me. I'm gonna have to never see you again.*

And I said, *Michael, that's ridiculous. We are family. What about my boys; you are their most fervently loved family, you are their uncle.*

And he said, *Well, I'm sorry, but I won't be able to see them anymore, either.*

And that, that right there, a kind of emotional extortion neither of us could have named or understood at the time, is when my stomach dropped out, and I said,

Wait! Let's talk about it.

Did we allow ourselves to believe it could be understood and therefore eventually embraced? I remember thinking at one point that the whole trespass might be experienced as a kind of relief, a relief to know that that stubborn cast iron beam there at the clumsy back of their twenty-three-year marriage had finally been confronted. And if not, then I was at least consoled that I had cleverly spared my own boys any of that post-divorce dating unbearableness that might've loomed up ahead had I not chosen familiar, beloved "Uncle Michael," and instead left them to encounter strangers traipsing through the kitchen in the mornings and rifling through the fridge hunting for eggs and toast. I was sure I had spared them at least that. But this queasy decision—to set the seesaw back in motion between two sisters with one man as the barrel hinge at the center—was too heavy, and under no circumstances, no matter the hierarchies or taxonomies, would it be experienced that way. I had spared no one, it had not been endured sturdily, and no literary figures were modeled and no part of it was turned into jokes.

There were no jokes to be made about it.

DECADES EARLIER WHEN this sordid story began, I shared with my father that I had just found out that my boyfriend and my sister had had a one-night stand, as they'd explained it, and my dad said, "Oh yeah, Gabs, that's been going on for a while." He had known, it turns out, that they were having an ongoing affair and had not told me. I felt like I'd been knee-capped; once by them but, secondly, by him especially, and I could not pack my passport fast enough. *With family like this* . . . I sportingly channeled a little Rodney Dangerfield humor, while racing to the airport.

But decades later, when the seesaw slammed down and I sent my own tender sister into the wilds of betrayal and stunned fury, our father at last intervened. He declared me dead to him. He didn't say this to me directly but announced it there at his favorite after-work bar, sipping a Negroni. The bartender later passed it along to Michael, who passed it along to me. I called my dad when I heard and left him a message at his office. "Hi, Dad. I hear through the bartender grapevine that *I am dead to you?*" I said it with a question mark. And then I giggled a little, at the melodrama of it. It's possible he never said it at all, that it was just an unsubstantiated rumor; given the clichéd wording I could see that as a possibility. But I was calling to confront him. To verify the data. To face my chores and shoulder my responsibilities. To show him the right way to disown me.

"Well. I'm sorry to have put you in that position or to have caused you to feel that way. Let me know, maybe, when you get a chance, in person. Better to hear it that way, I think, than through the bartender." How many times, I start to wonder, have I had to telephone this man to teach him how to be? It's outrageous, of course, to have behaved as I have and yet to feel entitled to find a moral failing in my father's response. I somehow cannot relinquish this relentless insistence that someone in the room must remain reasonable, in charge, focused, principled, must keep a steady hand on the rudder. Someone, I feel, must captain the ship and take care of the crew, even when the winds are whipping up, and I have an incorrigible sense that it should be him. This is before I am aware that I am now the wind. That I am the one *who troubleth his own house and who shall inherit the wind*. He did not return my call.

THE TERRIBLE SCANDAL that I had authored settled eventually into a plain and rather gentle fact of life to be lived, and we lived it privately and contentedly for its duration, of a couple more very pleasant years. It had been scandalous. Then, matter-of-fact. But even so, the town and the family and our relationship to both were unrecoverable. None more so than with Jeffrey, who lost in the explosion not only his anchor and dear friend, Michael, whom he could most certainly not forgive, but all the parties and the lamb roasts and the graduations and the cash advances and the free dinners and the swimming pools and the woodsmoke and the only front yard left in any of our lives that had held the feeling of home. The last place on Earth that had still held all of us—the argumentative and the provocative and the rivalrous and the violent and the discerning alike—surrounded by fireflies, in her cool pleasant shade. We had *blown it to smithereens,* as we would admit grimly, shaking our heads incredulously, as if we ourselves were shell-shocked bystanders and not the agents of the shelling.

WHEN JEFF DIED, my father was the one who mustered, in spite of everything, and left the voice message on my telephone. *Hello, New York. Dad here. Last night Jeffrey hung himself—"hanged" himself, I guess is how it's said. Anyway.*

That's over, he sighs. His voice is matter-of-fact, resigned. As if some inevitability has finally arrived. *I thought you should know,* he says, and hangs up.

In the course of thirty years of cutting off my mother, the general feedback is that there is something unreasonably angry and unforgiving about me. And until Jeffrey killed himself, and I heard my father say, "Well, that's over," in that shrugging tone of his, as if some humdrum old fate had finally come to its inevitable eventuality, I had never believed otherwise. I accepted myself as harsh. Strident. Demanding. I knew I was exceedingly difficult to love. Even harder, perhaps, to like. All of us, all of the siblings, have been described at times by those who know us as "prickly." I had always understood the question of familial rifts and estrangement to be about parents who cannot suffer one more minute of their insufferable children but who feel wounded and unduly punished when their children—who have picked up on this—remove themselves from the unbearable position in which they find themselves. Who leaves and who is left has been an enduring confusion for me for decades. "I hurt," I once heard a famous writer in an interview say, "which has two opposite meanings."

But hearing that phrase and that tone—"Well, that's over"—was the first time one of his doozies hit me as neither scintillating nor charmingly contrarian. It woke me, suddenly, like a middle-of-the-night click of a latch on a downstairs window.

The casual diagnosis we prized: unique, with the symptoms we favored—individualistic, complicated, straight-shooting; if you weren't complex, endowed with dark humor, unflinching candor, a robust constitution, and charming quirky eccentricity, you were then simple, small, mundane. A *clerk*.

But suddenly, retrospectively, we seemed obscene, tawdry, ugly, even dangerous. It started to seem to me that there might be something more egregious at play than bushy eyebrows and crowded teeth. Family drama and contentiousness and scandal seemed manageably colorful to me up until then—nothing *straight and narrow* here to scoff at—and, in some way, lent a veneer of intellectual or artistic bona fides to us; in the most enduring literature, and in the most regarded publications, writers insist on such complexity as if it were the Platonic ideal.

You know there is no such thing as a Norman Rockwell family, and you know equally well that it would reveal something cloying and facile about yourself—that you lack backbone and intellectual integrity—to admit to nonetheless longing for one. Since you were old enough to sit up at the table and use a fork and knife, you've read the faces and clocked the disappointed reactions when someone's plus-one at the dinner party, who won't soon be invited back, has blithely

> *recounted a long dream,*
> *wept sentimental sentiment,*
> *told a happy-ending story about their childhood,*
> *gushed immoderately about their own ordinary and*
>   *unexceptional children,*
> *expressed an earnest sense of hope,*
> *wept, without apologizing.*

I have all along studied the mistakes, the markers of having flubbed, whiffed, and screwed the pooch on intellectual and artistic rigor. And I have tossed around in my mind the Platonic, the Aristotelian, and the more flexible Wildean ideas of Life imitating Art and Art imitating Life. Have scrambled them all together at times, and perhaps foolishly also made room for the merits of the barstool wit and the dinner party raconteur. But sudden death, suicide, irrevocable family destruction, loss, and demise struck me as black and severe. This is not Art. Nor Anecdote. This is Life. Something to sit up straight and salvage what's left of.

In particular, my own life. The way I'd been rigging it, provoking it, pushing at the seams of it to see if it would bear my weight and announce my complexities. Divorced, rancorous, estranged from my family, with a preteen son who has already had detention and been suspended for bullying, who has howled his wish to emancipate by the time he's in sixth grade; my transgression, an affair with my own sister's husband, quickly and garishly picked up by Page 6, all of which had been admittedly problematic yet categorically permissible to me up until then as "a little messy" or "human" or merely "alternative." *Show me one person who doesn't have some complicated relationships,* I would've thrown down as a dismissive gauntlet back then—until my dad said about Jeffrey, hanging there dead, "Well, that's over."

I find myself listening to that voice message—as both a Hamilton parent and a Hamilton child—in sober alarm: *Am I perpetrator and casualty in the very same body?* I worry. I can no longer find anything funny or charming about who I've been or who I might be if, sitting here bolt upright in the dark, I don't throw back the covers, grab the bat, and go downstairs to confront the intruder. Who may very well already be deep inside the house.

I am invited to the wedding of a cherished employee of mine around this time. I have been this guy's employer since he was a twenty-year-old kid, and over the years have welcomed his young friends and his roommates to family meals and to festive Easter bonnet parties and to stray-dog Thanksgivings at my restaurant, and now he is in his thirties, getting married. I meet the father of one of his friends—a hard-hustling, witty, self-deprecating fireball of a kid who is growing up to be an outstanding gentleman—and I gush to the father about his wonderful, polite, well-bred, hardworking son, and the father takes my hand, thanks me, and, smiling with a real sparkle in his eye, says, "Well, the fruit describes the tree!"

MISTAKES WERE MADE

EVERY SPRING OF every year of my father's life—married, divorced, remarried, separated; at our childhood home, at the bachelor rentals, at his shore house, at his studio; on his deck, on his lawn, in raised beds, in tilled earth; one foot cut off at the ankle, then the leg cut off at the knee; one valve in his heart opened with a stent, then all four valves stented, and then again, yet another stent, this one placed in his groin; no matter: Every spring my father plants a garden. He starts the season with scallions, radishes, and snap peas and ends it with tomatoes and beans and Swiss chard. He is forever arriving at someone's house for dinner and, instead of flowers or a bottle of wine, presenting an artful but unadorned bouquet from his garden. Even if I haven't seen the man in years, no matter how long I've now been dead to him, in spite of the fact that he is now possibly months away from his own death,

I can picture exactly where he is on those warm sunny mornings as he thins his radishes and stakes his tomato plants.

One day, I arrive home late in the afternoon and find a slim box on the front stoop. Inside is a bouquet of green onions, radishes, lettuces, chives, and slender pale carrots; they arrive rolled up inside wet newspaper, perspiring inside a plastic baggie that has been delivered to the front door of my apartment all the way from his home in rural New Jersey. With no note and no return address. None needed; I recognize the gesture instantly. *Come on,* he seems to be saying. *Here is a wet newspaper cone of this year's first scallions and radishes from my garden. Stop being dead to me.*

I feel moved—a little—by this gesture, this subtle bid for a truce. It occurs to me for the first time that what he loved about our favorite movie is probably not what I loved about it: the stick-shift driving, cigarette smoking rascal daughter. And that more likely what he loved was the widow-swindling, grifter father who was never forced to say anything tender and who could disappear for years but still show up late and be loved by her. He is, and always has been, charming. But I don't reach out.

Instead, at work the following day I start running an item on the new spring menu: a pinzimonio—a small, neatly formed cone of wet newspaper stuffed with the season's earliest first crops from the farmers market, a few radishes and baby white turnips and a few scallions, sweet peas, and leaf lettuces—and serve it with a dish of first-press olive oil from Italy, a good flaky salt, and I tell the waitstaff to explain the newspaper cone, if anyone asks: *It's a thing from her dad. He used to always do that.*

About a year later, this time at the end of the season, I find in my mailbox a package with a bubble-wrapped jar of homemade bread-and-butter dill pickles; it's poorly sealed and the liquid looks cloudy. This time there is a note that says, *Mistakes were made. Hope you enjoy my latest project.* And he signs it, simply—*Dad*.

I put the murky jar of homemade pickles up on the bookshelf next to the urn that has our dog's ashes. I didn't know about Barry Goldwater when I was six, and he was teaching me about runners-up and also-rans. But I am in my fifties by now. I know who Nixon was. I know "mistakes were made."

I spend quite a bit of time in the following months chewing over this maddeningly unsatisfying, passive phrase—*mistakes were made*—and wondering if he actually thinks that'll do it. If that'll bring us back to life. A few charming words handwritten in his black felt pen, his architectural penmanship, meant to resuscitate. I suspect he has no inkling of how it landed on me, the dead daughter, to have been declared dead. Even I don't yet know how it has landed on me; I'm still making witty quips about it, giggling on the couch at the analyst's office, telling it as a joke at parties. As if it was funny and not itself lethal. "A jar of pickles!" I exclaim, giggling. "As if that'll do the trick!" The overtures he makes are dear, and approximate; here is a man, a father in the last weeks or months of his own life, who starts to feel the pinch of time, trying to bring his dead daughter back to life with wet newspaper and murky pickles. It's like he's wearing a Halloween-costume white lab coat and one of those big mirror things strapped to his forehead, fumbling the CPR, with his toy plastic defibrillator and a child's play-doctor rubber stethoscope. And here is his daughter, the actual life-sized patient—unimpressed, with her arms crossed against her chest; she has, unfortunately, long ago been made aware of high standards and the value of meeting them.

His efforts are oblique, offhand, and emotionally inexpensive; he does not spend the actual emotional capital it would take to bring his daughter back from the dead. He doesn't seem to want to exert himself. He seems more inclined to summon her in an aesthetic and gestural way. But to her it reads as amateur and half-assed, like instead of walking out to where she is buried to do the hard shoveling to exhume her—instead of getting back on that overturned mower, shaking, but professional—he is instead goofing around with a Ouija board with friends, sitting around in a squirmy candlelit séance, hoping for a signal.

And again, I do not reach out to him.

But then, some months later, he calls to make a reservation at my restaurant. He has spoken with my manager, who sends me a panicked text: *What should I do? He wants a brunch rezzie???* He is apparently not as near to death's door as I had imagined.

These parents, whom we count as down at least four or five times in their end zones, about whom we make urgent false-alarm calls to all the important people—"Better get here!" we say. "It looks like this is it, the end!"—but who then rise, astoundingly, and take walks in the hallways of their nursing homes demanding butterscotch candies from the nurses, who stand in their driveways hosing down their boats, who schedule their haircuts in time to be wheeled into a restaurant for a dry Manhattan—two cherries—and who blow out the candles on yet one more hard-to-believe birthday cake. I cannot be anything but proud of him and frankly awed: I thought he was as good as dead, but, apparently, he is back from the brink. He is thinking about coming into New York City and he wants brunch.

For this, I come back to life. I call him back. We don't take reservations for brunch. He answers.

"Hey, Dad. I heard you called for a brunch reservation. What is the occasion?"

"No, nothing special. Just coming in to see a matinee and I thought we'd stop for lunch."

I've had my restaurant some sixteen years by then; he's eaten there three times. We haven't seen or spoken to each other in the four years since Jeffrey killed himself, and this is the first conversation we are having, and it's about a brunch reservation. He's down to one leg, I've heard, and uses a walker.

"Dad, um, brunch is a real circus. What is the reason for your visit, if you don't mind my asking? Why is it important that you have brunch at Prune?" I ask again. "I can make you a reservation anywhere, if you'd like, someplace calmer and closer to the theater."

"Oh, nothing special, Gabs. Just going to a matinee and thought I'd have lunch at your place. We don't want any special treatment or anything."

There are over twenty-five thousand restaurants in New York City; to me it is mandatory that if he is to get what he wants then he must say what it is he is really after. Maybe it is the sixteen-hour restaurant days; the alternate-side parking of the car; the walking of the new dog; the increasingly complex needs of the two adolescent children; the thirty employees; the divorce; the writing deadlines; the two dead brothers; the exile from home, hometown, and family—self-imposed or otherwise—or the three days a week of hard, unflinching labor on the analyst's couch, but, whatever it is, I am unwilling to budge on this.

There's a section in the Berlitz phrase books for all the things you may want to say in languages you don't speak, phrases that can be used and uttered by anyone—phonetically—no matter their generation. They are just the letters that, when strung together, form the words that convey the sentiments. All you have to do is be willing to sound them out and commit to saying them. You don't have to be fluent. Or literate. You can buy a shirt, exchange foreign currency, eat at a restaurant, discuss the weather, get directions, tell the hospital doctor what's wrong, go on a date, go on a same-sex date, change a tire, ask to charge your iPad, you just have to have the will to say what you want to say.

I have only heard about his amputation but haven't seen it.

"Do you walk?" I ask.

"I get by," he says. "In very short bursts."

"I don't think it's a good idea, Dad. It's too crowded and chaotic in here during brunch." And we gently hang up.

I know I am gambling. It's a game of chicken—If he dies am I going to be okay? Is there anything I still need from him? Anything I feel I owe him? We all try to predict this about ourselves when we can see the end nearing. He's down to one leg. This is surely his last garden. His own death is coming soon— it's written. The when is still unknown, but it's coming. Whether or not I will miraculously spring back to life in time, if I will get a heartbeat and revive, if I will soften and relinquish my stance, if I will allow myself to be charmed by the representational, the metaphoric, the gesture of a murky jar of pickles, the perspiring radishes, the cryptic notes—this, too, remains unknown.

Part Four

COURAGE

JEFFREY HAD ALREADY been dead a full two years by the time I was nerved up and ready to call my mother to ask about the rumor that she had said No to him when he, as a last resort, asked if he could come and stay with her for a spell. He'd been remembered in obituaries and tributes in the local papers I'd found online, where they spoke of his youthful anthropological excursions—one to the Dordogne, and the one to Africa when he was only nineteen—and they noted that he spoke Swahili and French, was a supertaster and could identify everything in every dish he ate, and that he'd had a firewood-cutting business and did junk hauling in our home-town, where he'd come and clear out your estate and keep the treasures worth keeping for himself to be sold at his annual barn sales, before taking the rest to the dump. He did business as the Marquis of Debris, and there were some who knew him not by his given name, but simply as *the Marquis*. Each one noted his honesty and integrity, his intelligence and remarkable character, his one-of-a-kind-ness.

But there were no published facts. No data. No answers to the following questions:

Had he hung himself from a ceiling beam, a shower rod, or had it been from a tree?

Where was he found?

Who found him?

Where was he living at the time?

How did he get there?

And also, how did he get *there,* to such a point?

When he jumped, had he been wearing his smooth, flat, perfect turquoise ring? His brimmed hat?

For some reason it felt vital to either find the actual tree, if there'd been one, or know what he had been wearing, as if it would make everything else, all at once, known to me. Like when you figure out a key letter in a crossword puzzle or a game of hangman, and then suddenly you see it, the entire phrase.

I'd been living with all of my questions like a hoarder who lives with piled newspapers and bags of kitty litter. So crowded is my own mind with loose questions stacked on top of other questions that certain doors can't even open all the way.

Had she really said No?

After decades of cutting her off, I must call my mother. I'd been dragging my feet on this fact-checking phone call for months upon months. Like I'm stalling at the top of the high dive, staring down at the water below. It's one thing to have questions but another thing to be ready to accept the answers.

I was afraid she might, legitimately, say, *You don't speak to*

*me for what—thirty years?—and now you want me to take
your call and answer your questions? Go fuck yourself!*

On the day I finally manage to dial her number, it is early
spring, a hard and white daylight at the window. The phone
rings only twice before she picks it up. I do some figure-eight
pacing on the living room carpet.

I identify myself. "Hi, Mom, it's Gabrielle."

She lets out a little surprised "Huh!," confused and pleased
at once, then says, "My Gabrielle?" And then she starts howling with laughter.

"I know," I say. "Hard to believe."

And on she goes, riotous, operatic laughter. I picture her as
Snoopy on the top of his doghouse, with cartoon tears foun-
taining to the ground, teeth bared all the way to the gums,
holding his tummy, while on my end of the phone I grin a
closed-mouthed little sheepish smirk, like someone who has
come back to borrow more money. I'm relieved to find her precisely where I thought she would be: unfazed by my long absence and lavishly amused by her own sense of humor.

Her laughter settles into grinning. I still know the sounds
of her.

"Gabri, hello. What is the occasion for the call?"

"Well, I was hoping I could ask you some questions. I need
some information about Jeffrey's death, and about our family;
there is such a great deal of information I am missing."

"Oh. Yes. Of course." She sighs. "Oh dear. Well, Gabri,
well, I'll do my best. I'm a little fuzzy myself these days, you
know. Lots of things I find I can't remember anymore. Perhaps
selectively!" And here she cackles again, a big and hearty
laugh. I instantly recognize her and feel an unexpected affec-

tion for the good-humored way she has always delighted in the plain facts of her own human beinghood, even while maintaining a strict intolerance of ours. With us, she was stern and physically insistent:

Put on a sweater!
Enunciate!
Stand up straight!
Pick up your feet!
Stop sulking.
Hang up the phone.
Get off your ass!
Shut. Up.
Wake up!
Introduce yourself.
Don't be ridiculous.
Eat it.
Keep your voice down.
Stop being so dramatic.
Turn off that noise!
Stop walking like a truck driver.
Stop being such a pill!

But with herself she has always been permissive and humorous about her own controlling, demanding nature. "Put on a sweater, why don't you. *I'm* cold!" she'd joke—meant to let you know that she knew herself. Was self-aware. Like she is here now, pretending to have memory loss "perhaps selectively!" declared with crinkly eyes and a toothy smile.

"Well, Mom." An avalanche of questions is starting to

rumble at the top of my mind. "I'm just gonna dive in here, okay? Do you know where he was found? Or who found him?"

"Oh gosh, Gabri. I wasn't part of all of that. You might do much better if you called Dad and Melissa—they'll know all of that."

I sigh.

"Yes, I realize, but alas, that avenue is not available to me. As I am sure you know."

"I'm sorry I can't be more helpful there," she worries. "Did you know he'd been in rehab? And there'd been, I believe, a diagnosis of bipolar," she adds, trying to be useful and helpful in any way she can.

"I remember he used to really lay into you sometimes," I say.

Here she chuckles, and she describes one of Jeffrey's recent visits. She takes a certain delight in telling the story and lights up while telling it.

"Oh boy, did he ever give me a good going-over once up here on a visit to Vermont! I don't know if you ever heard about that one, Gabri. A three-hour *dissertation*." She leans heavily into the word, seeming delighted with her choice of vocabulary. "Shut down the dinner table that night, on his visit, telling me I was the *worst* mother in the *history* of motherhood!" She is laughing, highly amused. Maybe even boastful. Then she says, "I'm sure he felt much better after *that*."

"Yikes. That sounds pretty rough," I say. "He really let you have it."

"Oh no," she says. "That was just his take on things. He needed to get it off his chest."

With five of us in the rotation, it was a hallmark of her

entire life as a parent to have one or another of her children, even long after they'd become adults, at their wits' end with her, confronting her—apoplectic at what we called her "Teflon nonstick coating"—and then slamming down the phone, or getting back into the car, or pushing themself away from the dinner table and refusing to speak to her ever again, to visit her ever again, to stay even a full twenty-four hours in her company ever again. And a characteristic of hers, her whole life, to find our complaints impertinent and to shrug her indifference.

"*Tant pis,*" she shrugs, in perfect French, as the phone clicks dead in her hands; as she finds herself alone at the dinner table with the opposing chair thrown askew; as she is washed in the red taillights of the car as it reverses, then peels out; as she is left alone again at the top of her mountain driveway. Then, she says it again with a heavy put-on American pronunciation, purposely butchering the words, "tant-piss," and she laughs a haughty dismissal, goes back inside.

She has never taken any of us on, and I believe she is proud of this.

But I feel proud, too, in a way, to have spared us both at least one set of complaints: my own. One unanticipated outcome of being estranged for thirty years: I have never, actually, let her have it.

"BUT I FEEL like Simon was much more difficult," she continues. "You maybe don't remember, you may have been too young to remember, but Simon was kicked out of the house."

I keep the phone to my ear and my demeanor breezy at this

remarkable thing she has said, but I have to pace the den a dozen rounds here, oddly giddy with incredulity: My mother imagines it possible that I might not remember such an episode. Your father rolling open the rail-car door to Simon's tiny room in the warren, at the end of the narrow corridor, slanting sunlight suddenly streaming from his room, your brother being hauled by the neck of his T-shirt, stretching it out, then chased down the stairs; he hasn't had his growth spurt yet, his boyish blubbery hips and chubby tummy shaking as he runs like hell, taking the stairs three at a time, being chased out of the home. After a silent dinner the sun begins to set, and the pitch of night falls, and the windup clock goes round its set of twelve midnight chimes downstairs in the plant room. She now, at eighty-six years old, seems to find it possible that you might have been too young to notice or that you might have forgotten how you stayed awake shivering all night, in the thick of summer, nauseous at the gaping silence down the hallway where his bedroom was, at his flat, empty bed, every time you crept down the corridor and checked on his room to see if he'd somehow snuck back in, and, finding he hadn't, imagining in what ditch he lay dead. Noticing that no one was making phone calls, no one was stapling posters to telephone poles, no one was out driving around in the car, with the windows down, calling his name like you might for a lost pet dog.

"But Jeffrey," she continues, "I did not find difficult, no."

IT'S POSSIBLE SHE is proud of herself for being able to stand by unflustered, and to unflinchingly let her unhinged, agonized adult son spend three dinner table hours belligerently petitioning for his needs and demands and hurts and experiences to be atoned for, to be honored, to be contended with. It's possible she is proud of her ability to give him an audience: "I am sure he felt much better after that!" She projects a confident sense of herself as a correct mother, in what must have been a painful and emotionally charged evening. I imagine Jeffrey, a bottle of wine already finished and another in the works, unleashing on her at the dinner table—it must have been harrowing—but she is undisturbed as she tells the story in a way that suggests that she feels she has performed excellent Mothership. Sturdy and steady, demonstrating expansiveness and receptivity, she has been able to stand fast and let her little kitten scratch and mew as much as he wants or needs. And she won't take any of it personally, she will hold it steady, treat him like he is a sugar-loaded naptime child just having a tantrum and not like a fiftysomething-year-old adult who is in extremis over the way he feels he has been so poorly mothered, so egregiously and deleteriously uncared for. He can punch and punch and punch but she holds him at arm's length, by the forehead; she knows the old trick. She receives him as the mother she is while he spends three hours arguing, vituperatively, for the mother he needs.

She's amused a little in the retelling. She chuckles, even.

SHE SIGHS, FINALLY, now welling up, I can hear it over the phone. "Well, Gabri, I hope you'll never have to know it, knock on *wood*," she says. "There is no greater grief than the grief of a mother who has lost her child."

I give her the minute she needs before continuing. I notice

that I can even hear this platitude, this diminution of anyone else's grief and the aggrandizement of her own, without it riling me up, and I find her amusing, entertaining even.

"Mom, there's a rumor . . ." I finally say.

I float the question gently and with all of the context I can supply.

"I don't even know these people, Mom, who've suggested this, but . . . but there are some rumors out there that you said he couldn't live with you when he called for your help?"

"Oh. Well, let me get my calendar, would you?" And she drops the phone for minutes while she goes off into the wilderness of her cluttered life, her house, her kitchen, her stacks of papers, her archive boxes.

I stop pacing finally and sit at the dinner table with my laptop open, waiting for her to come back.

The last time I spoke to my mother, my oldest son weighed nine pounds and was swaddled in a striped hospital blanket, with those miniature cotton mittens they place over the hands so the babies don't scratch their own faces with their tiny new fingernails. On the day of this phone call he is in the process of applying to specialized high schools in New York; he is capable of crafting a coherent and persuasive five-paragraph essay using a sophisticated vocabulary. He is now a classic fourteen-year-old, which is to say a leading authority in our household on any subject that may casually come up: Shakespeare, karate, chess, sarcasm versus irony, Kanye, right-wing podcasters, DJ Khaled, smash burgers, counterfeit Louis Vuitton shower slippers, and the proper way to use a "chitarra" for making by hand his own pasta alla chitarra. On this day he is newly hyped to have discovered fencing, and I have earlier this morning gladly dropped him off for a few hours of practice.

The last time I spoke with my mother I had only this one son, the size of a capon. But now I have two, and the other one is upstairs in his room as I make the anxious phone call. He's a quick and intellectually astute middle-schooler who abhors waste and inefficiency and tardiness; I can hear him upstairs swearing impatiently into the microphone on his headset, glassy eyes reflecting the blue of the computer screen as he destroys some online opponent in whatever game he is currently obsessed with, voicing his disappointment in a teammate who has wasted something—a shot, an opportunity, his time. He reminds me, often spookily, of Todd.

My mother has never met him, never heard his voice. In the expanse of time it has been since we have last spoken to or seen each other, there are now these two human beings who have evolved through swaddling and diapering, finger painting, potty training, swimming lessons, spelling bees, summer camp, all the way up to and through report cards, detention, custody schedules, family therapy, a Great Lakes road trip with my new/old boyfriend who also happens to be their favorite beloved uncle, downhill snow tubing, Christmas mornings, and, most recently, a new apartment move-in with my new wife; they are now at the point that they can swipe a Metro-Card and ride the subway by themselves but mostly jump the turnstile instead because they think it's cooler. Even the younger one is now old enough that he can cook himself a bowl of tortellini after school when I am late at work. But somehow my mother is dropping the phone on her desk while she goes off in search of her notes as if I call every day at this hour. When she finally comes back and fumbles the phone to her ear, she has a calendar in front of her, and she leafs back through to the month and year that Jeffrey died, and then reads to me the recorded details of the dates in question. She uses the notes she carefully keeps on her calendars to keep her slowly flaking memory in fresh-coat-of-paint shape. When the fuel tank was last filled. When she ordered firewood. Who called her that day. And who she called that day. A few years later when I am going through her papers in her sunroom I will find today's calendar, and her notes on it: "Gabri calls! Long visit."

"Well, Gabri, I remember that I had immediately looked into my Medicaid package to see if his therapy and medication and medical care could be attached to mine.

"Here, it says, I wrote to myself, that I looked into a possible job for him at the Cabot creamery, making cheese and butter, but they weren't hiring. I didn't think I could care for him at my age and on my fixed income. So, I asked him not to come."

Two days after our phone call a photocopy of the page she'd been consulting arrives in the mail—she, too, is quick to let the fact-checker know, before being asked, that her story stacks up.

So, she had in fact said No.

I had been chickening out on this phone call for two years, not quite ready to hear this. And yet, it turns out to be a reasonable and comprehensible No. A decision made by an eighty-three-year-old woman living impossibly close to the edge on her fixed income of $13,000 a year—using the cardboard tubes from paper towel rolls jammed into the window frames to keep the cold drafts from rattling the panes in winter, holding her knee socks up with rubber bands when the elastics gave out, receiving government heating fuel assistance, plus Medicaid benefits. A decision made by a woman incapable—

she says she felt at the time—of receiving her burly, unpredict-able fifty-seven-year-old son, who had been recently diagnosed as bipolar and who had just checked himself out of his drug and alcohol rehab facility because, as he told her, he hated it and didn't "feel like himself there."

"I did recommend to him a book I thought he should read, that I thought would help—a wonderful philosopher—do you know him, Gabri? Montaigne? I find myself transcribing bits of his into my own common book . . . wonderful, deep, and probing thinking; I had hoped he might find some solace in that."

I get up to pace a little again and there is my twelve-year-old, at his bedroom door, urgently rolling his fingers at me to "wrap it up," to let me know we have to leave soon for some-thing I have agreed to drive him to. He does not do particu-larly well when made late by someone else's poor time management, and I tend to agree with him—my problems should not be his—so I quickly ask my mother if we can pause. If I can call her back, if not later that day, the next, or if not tomorrow another day.

"Mom, I think I already know the answer but, explicitly, would it be all right with you—may I call you at any time, whenever I want, as much as I want?"

"Oh, Gabri, of *course.*

"You don't even have to *ask.*"

And right behind that, she finishes with:

"I'm your *Mother.*" And we hang up.

So, it's true after all. She had said No. And it's also true that a few days later he killed himself. But it had not been the kind of horrible No the gossiper from our hometown sug-gests, in her casual email catching up with her old friend.

Still not smoking? Bravo for you, friend! Have fun in Ecuador—I'm sure your espanol is as good as ever!

Too bad about Jeff, but does it come as any surprise? I don't think he maintained a healthy lifestyle.

Our mother is now cleared of suspicion and no longer a person of interest for me. And she has no more data than I do, so she is no longer of use, even. Mostly, though, the conversation has gone so well, and I have found her so pleasant and funny and bearable that I don't ever want to call back, in case it was just a stroke of beginner's luck. I want my final exchange in life with my mother to have been this positive one, to remember her by.

But a new question has come up overnight, and it nags at me enough that I find I must hazard the chances, and call her back, to follow up. She picks up the phone, this time not laughing as I identify myself; instead, she sounds as if she is sitting up straight, buttoning up. Perhaps herself unsure if it was beginner's luck the first time and perhaps also not wanting to flub the sophomore attempt.

"I'm calling because I was wondering, did you find yourself feeling guilty about that, later, when you got the news? I could imagine that being hard," I say.

"No, Gabri, I felt rather proud of him."

"Proud?" I have to blink away some confusion, to remain calm. Neutral. Curious. I'm suddenly back on the high dive, not ready for the answers.

"Yes. I feel proud of him in a way. To have had such courage to put an end to his anguish."

WHO AM I TO SAY?

WHO AM I to say it wasn't courageous? Who am I to say that he didn't square his shoulders in defiance, that he didn't take a brave and courageous stance by ending his anguish, by offing himself? Who am I to disagree with her? I'm the one, after all, who for a time imagined it as aesthetic, humorous, cleverly arranged, puckish. Why not courageous?

Who am I to say that it wasn't, as others seem to have felt, just a matter of time, a consequence of an unhealthy lifestyle, an inevitability awaiting its fated moment until it could be finally announced, "Well, that's over"? Who am I to say?

THE MARQUIS OF DEBRIS

LIKE MY MOTHER, in the absence of data or eyewitness accounts, I am left to my imagination, and I have imagined him out in the deep Pennsylvania woods searching with measured care for an appropriate tree. Like her declaring him courageous, I have thought, similarly, *Oh, that amazing guy; thorough and meticulous to the very end!*

Of all the ways to imagine his suicide, I have also chosen the optimistic. I had him in my mind's eye hanging himself in the bright afternoon, from a tree I envisioned as almost cinematically gorgeous. I imagined him auditing those trees, taking a long walk among them to decide on The One—the choicest one of those trees we all grew up in, around, under.

Those trees we knew so well, as if they themselves were siblings or neighborhood friends we used to pass the days with, digging forts and squirrel traps around the roots of.

Hiding and seeking among.

Home-basing.

Rubbing our bare legs with the rough, oily black walnuts they dropped, to release from them the citrusy compound that repelled the bloodthirsty mosquitoes when we played flash-light tag.

I had him, in my imagination, hanging himself from one of those familiar trees, the one that he had deemed worthy of such an intimate event, and then I imagined him being kept steady and gentle company for the rest of the afternoon by all the magnificent others rooted nearby.

I imagined him gripping his straw hat against the blinding sun.

Carrying a fine leather noose.

Dressed in corduroy, or selvedge denim, his mesmerizing flat blue moon turquoise ring on his finger.

Like her, I have thought my own version of "courageous." I have thought: How smart and how very like him that he went out and sought an exceedingly familiar place—the woods. How perfectly characteristic that he was not violent or gory about it—with a gun or a razor blade; that he was not discour-teous to others by leaving himself in a hotel bathtub for some poor cleaning woman to discover; that he was not disruptive or malicious by throwing himself onto the train tracks in front of a fully loaded railcar of tourists enjoying the quaint chugging-and-whistling two-mile excursion on our home-town's historic steam engine. I have even thought: How hilari-ous! A borderline OCD guy who needs ninety minutes to accomplish a complete shower that includes flossing, a profes-sional woodsman who argues the subtle differences of branches, heads into the woods to pick out a suicide tree . . . oh my god, that's funny!

Like my mother, I imagined all this in the void of not knowing where he was actually found, or how it actually happened.

UNLIKE MY MOTHER, I have no way of knowing how it really happened. She can just pick up the phone and get the full story by calling my sister or my father. But curiously, she sounds unmotivated to seek the information.

"Do you want me to keep you in the loop? Would you like me to share anything should I find it? I'm going to continue trying to track it down, I guess, the logistics and the details," I say, as we are hanging up.

"Oh." She pauses to think this over. "Uh, no, Gabri, I think I have everything. At eighty-six years old I don't think I can retain much more in this brain!" she jokes, cheerfully.

But tracking down the details leaves me feeling like a small unwelcome person at the back of a tall and broad-shouldered crowd, one who can't see who is speaking up front and who must keep tapping the backs of the strangers in front of her to ask them to relay to her what's going on. *What did the speaker just say? What is the commotion up in front? Suicide by hanging? Where? When? Who found him?*

In effect, I find myself learning what little there was available to know about the unexpected suicide death of my own brother by reading about it in the local newspaper, just like anybody else might have. And to wonder what portion of it was mine to account for.

Perhaps by dint of the fact that I don't have access to the data, I find myself preoccupied by its absence. It becomes a hunt, and I become a hound in pursuit. I like my imagined vision of his demise, but I'm conditioned now by the fact-checkers, the four separate editors, the analyst. Even I want to root out my own mistakes, to proofread my own imagination and correct the errors. I continue to seek the information haphazardly, indiscriminately, far and wide, low and slow, venturing into stagnant pools and fresh streams alike, hunting for the people— any person other than my father and my sister—who might be willing to talk to me and who might know the particular few basic facts. *What exactly happened here?*

I receive a phone call at work from someone who identifies himself as "an old friend of Jeffrey's" who says he saw him on the night before he died and who has a message to give me. He asks to meet me at a train station in Pennsylvania. I have booked a room at a nearby motel. Outdoor pool. Pet-friendly. My kids will love the breakfast buffet and the waffle station at least, if this turns out to be a bust. I arrive early and park in the train station lot, a few rows back from the station house. I take a walk around first, bring my new dog—a pit bull—just in case I need to show force, but have left the kids at the pool with the babysitter. There are signs posted—SUICIDE WATCH— with an 800 number to call because people hurl themselves onto the tracks. I can't help but split open laughing at such irony.

The guy arrives on the station platform, and I immediately know it's him—he has hair clippings in the cups of his ears and a couple of bloody nicks from a fresh shave when we meet. He is shaking a little. I wonder if he has an ankle tether under his pant leg—if he's on a day pass from his halfway house after twenty-one months in state prison for DUI—meanwhile, he wants to tell me that they'd had drinks together at the Candlewyck Tavern the night before Jeffrey decided "to go," and that when Jeff drove off in his big blue truck that night, he knew something wasn't right.

"But Jeff wanted me to be sure and tell you that he loved you!" Then he holds out his hand to take mine and asks, "So are you and I friends now?"

I giggle. "Umm, sure, I guess, if that's how this works," I say, taking my hand back to reach down to pet the dog's head and scratch her neck. Thanking the guy for his message, I get in my car and get out of that parking lot as fast as I can, groan-screaming out loud to myself in the car—*Oh my fucking god, oh my god, oh my god!!!!*—at the absurd places this hunt leads me. At the lying liars I have met along the way. Even I know that Jeffrey's big truck had been sold off long before his suicide.

I muster the courage to arrange a phone call with my brother Simon. He starts talking immediately, starts not at the beginnings but in the middles of sentences, and doesn't stop for forty-four minutes. I find him wildly upbeat, cheerful, talkative. I wonder privately if he has discovered Ritalin or Adderall but am shy to ask. Whatever it is, I find him indestructibly, if chemically, good-natured. Unencumbered by and distinctly uninterested in bringing up our own very remote past.

Water under the bridge.

Live and learn.

Let it all go.

Life's too short, man.

He works in easy T-shirt slogans, what some call bumper sticker wisdom. I've asked if I could talk to him about Jeffrey.

He launches into a description of a miserable week he spent with Jeff near the end that cost him a lot of money.

"Three thousand dollars, Gabs, by the time I got him his ticket and all of his meals and hotel rooms!" he exclaims.

He had flown Jeff out West hoping to offer a salutary reset, a healthy restorative week or two, thinking that some fresh air, some change of scenery, some time in natural California splendor would do him good. Apparently, Jeff had been depressed and had been forced to sell his truck because he needed the cash. And Simon—of all the family—was the one who had stepped up. I'm struck by the kindness and the generosity of his effort, and I recognize this strange and contradictory truth about all of us: At various times and in different ways, each one of us has gone to great lengths to rescue another, even though we harmed one another, erupted at one another, pummeled the shit out of one another. Even so, we have, each one of us, on dire occasion, tossed a rope to pull one or another out of the soup.

A very early memory: I don't know what he had done to provoke Jeffrey, but there they are, suddenly in a full explosive beating, Simon maybe six, maybe ten, Jeffrey maybe twelve, maybe sixteen, I'm too young to know the difference. The saliva, the teeth, the tears, Jeffrey's fists thudding against the thick body of the little boy, the squealing quality of Simon's crying. I'm a very small girl and can do nothing about it but stand there howling at the top of my lungs in protest, helpless, unable to intervene, screaming at the egregious unfairness, at the injustice of the imbalance in their sizes and weights, their ages, and at the merciless volatility of Jeffrey's unbridled violence. Even if Simon had stolen something out of Jeffrey's room, even if he had borrowed something without asking; I couldn't get over the he-doesn't-stand-a-chance-ness of it. And I have to imagine Simon couldn't, either.

And yet here is Simon now saying he had flown Jeff out West at his own expense to see if it would help. Finding Jeff prone to going off on rants on everybody and everything, he discovers he can barely wait to put him on a plane and fly him back East.

When I ask him to reminisce about some earlier experiences, ones from our early childhood that I'm myself still trying to be sure I have remembered accurately, he adds a few good lively bits, and has some corrections—"Oh no, Gabs, he didn't just drag that deer back to the house. He stuck his finger up its warm ass on the side of the road, to see how long it had been lying there!" He bursts with his own amazed laughter.

Simon has a laugh that makes me think of gasoline, and here he erupts at the scatological image of Jeffrey probing the deer to determine how long it had been dead.

"What about the one, did you ever know that time he caught a snake out back in our meadow? Squeezed it at the neck and five mice came rolling out? Yeah, Gabs! And he used the snakeskin to make himself a belt!" He sounds thrilled and impressed. I recognize in him the same pride I had had myself in the fourth grade, of being able to brag about Jeff to my classmates. "Pygmies! On an elephant hunt! Eats termites fried in palm kernel oil and swears they taste just like french fries!"

But just before we hang up, as we're winding down, he says, "Yeah, Gabs, you know Jeffrey hated you, right? Thought you were selfish. Awful. The whole bit. Hated Mom. Hated everybody."

That little sliver of candor, offered at the last minute as we're wrapping up his forty-four-minute stream-of-consciousness monologue is offered as a question. *You know he hated you, right, Gabs?*

He delivers it like an impartial courtroom stenographer, as if he has been asked to read back the record, as if he were merely the valet carrying the wax-sealed envelope on the velvet pillow from the king of one country to the queen of another, a trusted aide, enlisted to get the message to the sister.

And my automatic knee-jerk answer, even though I didn't know:

"I really do. Yes. I know. Thanks for telling me, Sime." I shorten his name, use the affectionate "Sime," as if I am coolly refolding the note and returning it to its envelope, unshaken, thanking the messenger for his faithful service.

The details that I do wish to know—where was he, who found him, how did it happen, where did it happen—it turns out Simon doesn't know, either. He was angry at Jeffrey at the end—felt he really tried to help him out, and at great expense, but was rebuffed; and consequently, he wasn't especially interested in the details of the final moments. "He was such a prick to me. And so negative about everything," he says, and we finally hang up.

Every cul-de-sac, dead end, and false witness forces me to cast my line farther, wider, and weirder. I land the thing in unlikely dark and far corners that yield next to nothing. I dredge the muddy bottom of the small pond of friends of friends of friends; follow dubious leads to people who live in the area, who somehow may be still loosely connected to my family and my hometown and to the "scoop" that might've been circulating if you'd been in the wired circuitry at the time

NEXT OF KIN   *211*

of his death. And from this uncertain and unvetted and unreliable bog, I reel in stranger and stranger phone calls, emails with snippets of gossip, some random videos; it's like going fishing and hooking rusted bicycle handlebars and a license plate after a twenty-minute battle with what you thought was a huge striped bass.

There's a literary event someone has recorded, some kind of public reading, and Jeffrey is in the video, he is one of the featured writers, at the podium. I estimate it as somewhere in the last five years of his life. He reads from his Africa journal. He introduces himself and then his work, and he points out that his book is still in print; I roll my eyes. Maybe I've gotten pouty after this news that Simon has dutifully relayed, maybe I've become extra critical and less enthralled by Jeffrey.

I talk back to the screen, even, like a heckler. "You mean your self-published book? You mean, you went over to Kinko's and printed a few more copies?" And crack myself up at my own amusingness.

He opens the pages before him on the lectern—they have brought in a lectern—and he begins:

The longer we stay
The more we realize
The less we know.

At first I pause, giving myself a minute to check my immediate wish to burst out laughing—thinking that it's so simplistic and so tenth-grade poetry class that it *must* be deeper, that it is a trick, one of those moments where you think, *Am I being punked?* But his friends in the audience hoot and holler and clap uproariously. Like the bearded sage has just blown their minds. Revealed the space-time continuum.

It's indecent, my response. I feel so mean ridiculing his scene. But I can't stop myself.

And then, letting the fact of it sink in, I grimace—*Oh, big beautiful brother. Jeffreaque. What have you done to yourself these past many years?*

In the local paper, separate from his obituary, someone has written a tribute, and they refer to him as an "icon." A "fixture on the landscape" of our hometown. "Much loved . . . highly regarded . . . unique . . . defied labeling . . . a renaissance man . . . wonderful person . . . great friend . . . ran a world-class debris business." I don't recognize the byline of the writer. Nor the names of Jeffrey's friends he mentions. It's absurd, of course, to imagine that in the decades that have passed he would still have the same friends I remember him having in his twenties. But I do wonder where they all have gone.

Right after he died, some of these new friends had thrown an all-day, meandering memorial-cum-celebration party in his honor, and videotaped the whole thing. The result is a little shaky and muffled in places, but a lot of people took the microphone and spoke their remembrances. There was laughter and fondness and there was a solemn bagpiper and plenty of beer and wine and a banjo player later that night as the pigs roasted and the sun set. Someone had sent me a link to this unabridged, unedited, meandering memorial video, and I'd watched it, pausing and rewinding, pausing and rewinding —perhaps 130 times that winter. I did not know most of the people in it—I had to constantly pause so I could fully examine their faces, their voices, their clothing, their gestures, as if in them there may be clues to who Jeffrey had become, who he'd been at the time of his death.

A friend comes into the frame—he's wearing a black bandanna tight on his head like a pirate, has beautiful eyes, a lot of heavy silver jewelry on every finger—and he reminisces about what it was like to run into Jeffrey and to share a spontaneous meal with him, recalling that he always had greasy lips with bits of food stuck in his problematic teeth. That he held his conversations while eating, while chewing.

He was a habitual surprise dinner guest. With impeccable timing. Always stopping by just as the meal was served, and laughing at the perfection of his timing, everybody jumping up from the table and pleased at his unexpected arrival. After much good-natured ribbing about how he must've smelled the roast roasting all the way down the driveway. And must have intuitively suddenly felt that now was the precise moment that he needed to stop by to deliver the wood, or drop off the keys, or come to see if he could pick up his check. He was always invited, warmly, to stay. "Pull up a chair, Jeff!" He wants so much to join but only if he can come correct. After all, he was not expecting this, and he has no bottle of wine in hand as hostess gift, and he must express his concern—*I know I'm stopping by without calling, I just now realized, of course, it must be your dinner hour, I'm so sorry, I'm really not expecting you to feed me, I totally understand if I'm interrupting—* which was met by every host, every time, unfailingly, with an extra table setting, bottles proffered and the meal rejiggered to include him. This he accepted wholeheartedly and with full-bodied eagerness. "Well, if you're offering sincerely then, yes,

I'd love to join you. I do not mind if I do! This looks superb!" He lets out his lion's roar, laughing at his immense good fortune.

And what an appreciative eater. Slow, methodical, dwelling on every crumb, crust, and bone. Every wingtip crunched and sucked and swallowed, every drop slurped, sometimes even licked from the bottom of a dish. Even apple cores, cheese rinds, dry heels of bread left in the basket; down the hatch with careful chewing, finger sucking, and fervid appreciation.

Such meals require two or three hours for him to fully relish and are followed always by embarrassed public flossing—he doesn't excuse himself from the table because he doesn't want to leave the conversation, so he flosses right there at his seat, apologizing. Poor us, the whole clan. Our family inheritance: intense dental overcrowding, making our lifetimes an unrelenting concern of picks and brushes and floss and Sensodyne toothpaste and protruding canines and receding gums and leaving all of us with some combination of a graying root canal and a small bridge or a discolored cap or a loose crown or half a dozen silver fillings.

From cuspid to cuspid, we are recognizable from a table length away. As my own orthodontist jokes, "Your teeth enter the room before you do!" At the end of every meal, he must floss.

Another guy comes onto the screen; he's missing a hand. As a high schooler, I think I remember hearing he'd blown it off with fireworks. He is now, forty years later, looking goth, skinny, in a black T-shirt and tight black jeans. He speaks of Jeff's intelligence and admires the heights and the fastidiousness of Jeff's mind. "I'm just saying, let's not forget that he was smart." And he backs off screen. Then another guy takes the mic, he's swept his long hair up into a man bun, and he wears his silky shirt unbuttoned in a deep V on his bare chest, and he lampoons Jeff's routine when meeting someone new, Jeff's obsession with getting names right, Jeff's fixation with spelling as the surest path to proper pronunciation, even with names that were simple.

"What's your name? Katie? Is that Katy with a *y* or Katie with *i-e*?" The gathered friends all gut-laughing with recognition. I am not laughing. I find myself wanting to button his buttons and scissor off his man bun.

A friendly young woman cheerfully describes her brief stint working for Jeffrey to help him organize his stuff. Everybody in the audience laughs roundly when she says, "He needed a *lot* of help getting organized."

They all know exactly what she means.

She describes in disbelief how his notes were written *on paper napkins*! That he kept *a manual address book*! and *didn't have a cellphone*! Three exclamation points of disbelief in a row as she memorializes him. But to me, where I am sitting at the dining room table poring over this video, I find him utterly recognizable and completely comprehensible—our father comes immediately to mind as I watch this woman gently ridicule Jeffrey. Our dad who rarely watched *the tivvies,* as he called the television, who instead read the newspaper, who left his car key under the floor mat of his car with his doors unlocked, who held his reading glasses around his neck with soft cotton butcher's string, whose purposeful insouciance was studied, practiced, intentional. Like Jeffrey's.

JEFFREY HAD A full thick head of hair yet always wore a hat, a wide-brimmed straw hat in the summer and a stiff felt one in the fall. He clipped and filed his fingernails meticulously, had lean forearms and slender ankles, with a stout rotund belly. He used to use his protruding gut as a playful weapon, to the squealing delight of the children he knew—mock smothering his nieces and their screaming friends with his hard-packed bloated belly and making monster noises, calling himself sometimes Uncle Billy, other times Fester the Molester. As kids we carried pillowcases from house to house to collect trick-or-treat candy, and shrieked with hysterical laughter when he leapt out from behind a tree or a hedge.

His conversation was earnest and ranging. Even forty years after he'd accomplished it, he still told the stories of his adventure in Africa. But he was quick to laugh at himself and his naïveté, was curious about the experiences of others, and he made the table where he sat feel alive and jovial, not deathly as if some self-involved monologuist was sucking the oxygen out of the room by holding forth about themselves. Everyone remembers how meticulously honest he was, with notes kept fastidiously of what work he owed people and what last parts of jobs he had left incomplete due to all the usual plagues that plagued him—his forever-breaking-down truck, his losing track of time, his need to stop the work to have a complete lunch with wine, the earlier setting sun or the rain squall—unexpected—that had left him unable to mow the grass or stack the wood at the agreed-upon time or date. But he never lost track of what he owed. He claimed to love to work in the woods late into the night and to enjoy, if not even to prefer, to split wood at night in the dark. He insisted that unless it was a completely moonless night he could see just fine. That his customers may have wanted to receive their cord wood in the daylight, neatly stacked, or have their estate cleared in the two days he had bid and not the seven days he had eventually needed and billed for, was an eccentricity of his for them to negotiate but, usually, they decided to hire him anyway, on his reputation for unwavering honesty.

The host and organizer of this celebration finally takes the microphone and welcomes everyone, thanks everyone for coming, for sharing. He has changed into a clean black shirt from his dirty apron and dirty T-shirt. His eyes are bloodshot, and he has a cigarette burning down in his thick dirty fingers. He is visibly moved. Emotion or fatigue or smoker's rattle— I can't tell—is in his throat and I can no longer go back to discern which; someone has overnight replaced the unedited video with a significantly cropped version. If I remember correctly, from my repeated obsessive viewings, he's been tending the whole roasted pig that will be the centerpiece of the reception to follow.

His story of Jeffrey is a story about himself and his own decency. Jeffrey is found "sleeping" at a party. "He was absolutely famous for showing up to parties three hours late, and while everyone was drinking and having fun, he would fall asleep on the couch!

"There was one party, though, where Jeffrey fell asleep and some people wanted to write on him with Sharpie marker!" Everyone in the audience groans. "They thought it would be so funny. But I protested, and I protected Jeffrey. I said, 'Aw, c'mon, guys, he is the Marquis of Debris, you can't draw on him with Sharpie.' I wanted to respect and honor his status, you know." Did he then look to the assembled group for affirmation, sitting on folding chairs on someone's lawn by the river, and did the group applaud, drink a toast, hold up their plastic cups? *Cheers, Jeffrey!*

Rest in peace, brother! To the Marquis of Debris!

I'm at my computer at the dinner table, this moment has been cut from the new edited version, it is lost, but I am still nonetheless curdling with shame and disbelief and embarrassment. Who "falls asleep" at a party? Was he just that tired, having pushed himself to keep going even after that long lunch, that clearing the woods in the dark, that splitting the wood by moonlight? Or, I feel myself squirming, had he gotten so high, so drunk, so fucked up that he passed out in front of everybody, like a stooge?

MOSTLY I RECOGNIZE the man they anecdotally reveal. The man who refused a cellphone, who kept his notes written on paper napkins, who was fastidious with names, who ate with gusto and appreciation, often enjoyed wine at lunch, who kept meticulous track of his debts and who incrementally repaid every cent of them, who had been fiendishly clever at sports and games and puzzles and wordplay, who was always telling good stories—a raconteur—even while eating. Even the friend who had been one of Jeff's landlords, who gently but frankly described Jeffrey as a hoarder, and who revealed that Jeff hadn't paid rent in something like eight years when he had lived on his farm, even this Jeffrey I recognized. I could see the person I knew in all of their testimony.

But even after a hundred watchings of this memorial, I couldn't connect the brother I had known with the people here who had gathered to remember him. Everybody already half buzzed in the afternoon, ineloquently telling one boozy, juvenile story after another about his eccentricities, evoking Jeffrey as the butt of the joke in anecdote after anecdote to their great general laughter and condescension. Had he become this, in the end? A greasy-faced, freeloading, pass-out drunk who couldn't manage a cellphone, or return a borrowed book, or properly credit the work of others, or even get through the day without losing his way and guzzling a bottle of wine, and skipping out on rent, and arriving several hours late to whatever he was invited to? Had he become the kind of guy who, even as he was nearing his sixties, still went to parties with the kinds of companions who think that drawing on a passed-out person with Sharpie is clever humor? Had he?

A lady at the end comes into the frame and tells a story that will leave me forever unsure—was Jeffrey the Jeffrey I knew, the masterful jester who was forever having a laugh on you, or was he the Jeffrey they seemed to know, the local idiot, now hanging from a branch, while everyone in town gathers, beer in hand, laughing at his fragility? Her final story knocks me off my feet, sends me sliding around on deck, from railing to salty railing.

She says The Soup was meant to be thrown away.

She'd made a big pot of soup one weekend and then, eventually, had shoved the leftovers, still in the pot, to the back of the refrigerator, and left it there, forgotten. And she worked around the pot of festering soup by shoving it to the side and ignoring it until she had the time and the fortitude to take it out and deal with whatever bubbling rotting brew she found. It had been fermenting in its large pot for so many months that she couldn't even throw it away; she had to just, in a fit of revulsion, carry the soup—pot and all—out into the snowy yard and let it sit there until spring, when she finally called for help. And she called her dear old friend Jeffrey, the Marquis of

Debris. And Jeffrey came and removed the putrid, festering pot—put the whole thing in the back of his truck and drove off. And she is standing in front of the gathered mourners and memorialists, holding the microphone, when she comes to her punch line. "And my phone rings a couple weeks later and it's Jeff, and I thank him for his help, and, at the end, he says, 'By the way, thank *you* for that delicious soup!'" Everyone assembled bursts into shrieks of revolted laughter. The groaning and laughing go on for unbearable minutes, it feels like, to me, home at the dining room table, pause and rewind, pause and rewind, pause and rewind. Rage seeping from my every pore.

THE CHARACTERISTICS WE SHARE:
>   *the need to wash washing machines*
>   *and hose down garden hoses*
>   *and to even out our shoelaces before tying them*
>   *the tendency to hoard*
>   *the particular depths to which we both test our father*
>   *bean counting and ledger keeping*
>   *steroidal hyper-honesty*
>   *doing physical outdoor work in the night in the dark*
>   *constant micro-accounting of perceived minuscule debts*
>   *owed to others*
>   *chronic apologizing for eating slowly and needing to*
>   *savor*
>   *for having to repeatedly ask the waiter to not clear my*
>   *plate yet because I am yes, still, unbelievably, still*
>   *eating*

the fear of misspelling or mispronouncing your name
chronic frictions and falling-outs with old friends we hold
    dear
the embarrassment over any single detail we may have
    accidentally overlooked

The unwelcome question starts to percolate hard and to finally break the surface: If this is what became of Jeffrey, is this what is in store for me? Is it just a matter of time? Will it be me next who is going to suddenly drift over the border between Eccentricity and Mania, who will find herself recently discharged from a hospital with nowhere to go, and who will just get up in the middle of the night and get in her car in the locked garage with the engine running, to be dead before sunrise? Will I be the next one of the least-liked children found dead in the morning, about whom our father will say something characteristically potent and candid, shrugging at the dinner table surrounded by his guests, *Well, I never understood how people put up with her anyway.*

When you are unpacking and cataloging the roadkill remains of your own brother's animal body, sticking your own finger up the warm ass of your hometown, his recent friends, the local papers, the strange emails and absurd phone calls and sad videos—scrubbing the area for DNA samples—all of these possibilities are considered.

I'M VISITING MY hometown quietly, still looking for answers, when I run into the mayor. I stay in a hotel, go about my business, avoid anywhere I think my father or my sister might be. I've been treading somewhat more boldly than usual; I'm not cavalier about what I've done, but still, I've begun to humbly, retrospectively stand by it. Things were already long broken, I've come to think.

The mayor has an antiques business, and I stop by his shop—it's been a family favorite for decades. Old estate crystal and sets of silverware, moss-covered birdbaths, trellised ironwork, sections of salvaged fencing and gates to old formidable manors. Enough time has passed that the scandal has come to be, if not forgiven, at least shruggingly dismissed; the mayor is friendly to me—like old times—when he sees me come into the shop.

"How're things up in New York?" he asks.

I mention that I'm interested in knowing what happened to Jeffrey's actual body. And that I've been wondering: Where is the Actual Tree? I want to know where he was found, what tree he picked to hang himself from, what he was wearing, who found him, what possessions he had with him, in what town was the police report filed, was there a crime scene in the days following, who called my dad and told him, which funeral home did the work, where is the death certificate, and, most ardently, what did the woods look like. Really that is what I want to know. I want to walk the path he walked and follow his steps, and I want to arrive at the very tree at the very time of year and at the same time of day he did, and I want to see what he saw. I'd like to close the book on this long period of fruitless questioning. To somehow cover and protect his body with dirt, in my own mind. The mayor jingles the change in his chino pockets, chews minty gum, slowly mulls over what I'm after.

"Huhn." He's thinking.

Then, in his heavy Philly accent—*wooter* for water—he says, "Can ya gimme a day or two?" He winks at me warmly, to indicate that he can almost certainly arrange something for me, given his stature in the town and the strings he can pull. He promises to get back to me if he finds out anything. He thinks he can pull a favor. And he goes to make a phone call. He knows the director of the funeral home where Jeffrey's body was dealt with. And only now, after entertaining several absurd years of gossip and unreliable testimony, and dead ends and meetings at train stations and drunks and high school wild cards and rotten soup, at *rope's end*, as Jeffrey himself would have punned, it at last occurs to me that I know him, too. *It is my home fucking town after all.* How many funeral directors can there be in Hobbitsville? Do you have to be the mayor to get the information or can you just be the little sister? I wonder.

NEXT OF KIN

I T TURNS OUT I can simply pick up the phone and call the funeral home mentioned in the obituary.

The information is available to the Next of Kin. Why this hasn't occurred to me for entire long slow-moving years is a brain problem, perhaps a buildup of plaque in the deep grooves of the neural pathways. I have up until now been stubbornly, in spite of the practical data, in the habit of thinking of myself only as someone intimate, as someone still on the inside: Family. I'd been operating all this time under the assumption that if I was ever going to get the information I needed, or if I was going to be allowed to attend the funerals and the memorials and the burials of our deceased, I would have to be invited, granted special readmission—in accordance with our own private particular familial procedures and bylaws. And I feared that I would have to bring myself to my father and my sister—in some ceremony of contrition, which I didn't have the stomach for, meted out in the great hall of my hometown. I thought that without their gracious invitation—without one of them going around town making my reinclusion *ostentatiously, publicly, formally condoned*—I was simply at an impassable impasse, with no way in.

It didn't occur to me that I could've simply recognized myself as the technicality I'd been for some time already, and that I could use my downgraded technical status to ask for the official record and be legally entitled to it. It did not occur to me that my rights were more intact and robustly guarded by the State's Statutes than they were by the moral code of my own mind, my own family, which had had me convinced that I'd forfeited them. It turns out you do not have to be honorable or pleasing or good-natured or successful or humble or hardworking or faithful or witty or have an immaculate character.

To get the official record,
You only have to be related.

Because I am Next of Kin, the funeral director tells me, I am allowed to know everything I want to know. This is a relief, though a joyless one. It cuts the mark where I stop being a Bone. I am no longer Gabbies, Gabri, Smella Fella von Gella, Prune, Pruney, Prunikins, Precious Nunu, and I have become, instead, a mere legal entity. In the same way that Junior, J Jasper, Fester, Uncle Billy, Jeffreaque, is now, simply, a cold and technical "decedent." I feel a little like I am breaking and entering when I request the documents, and again when I receive them, even though I am legally entitled to them. But I do not trip any alarms.

I am required to ask my questions through sanctioned legal channels and to follow protocols already in place for such circumstances. The funeral director tells me he is obliged to direct me to the county medical examiner's office. From the county medical examiner's office, I request and receive the autopsy report. The autopsy report leads me to the township police department. From the township police department, I request and receive the incident report. From the incident report, I learn there was a friend who found him, and her phone number is printed there on the report, and I learn there are photos available, upon separate request.

I stumble on this for some time. Then, I decide not to request the photos. The truth I seek is subtler, less graphic. And obviously, my imagination is active enough.

Instead, I decide to drive to "the decedent's" every known address for the past twenty years. Gas in the car. Notebooks. Pulling up into daunting driveways—derelict homes, abandoned cars, moss and mildew clouding the windows, the woman with heavy gravel in her chain-smoking voice when I call for verification: "Hello, ummm, my name is Gabrielle Hamilton and I am Jeffrey Hamilton's youngest sister. And it says here on the police report that you are the friend who found Jeffrey and I was wondering if I might see the tree? Would it be possible, if not too upsetting for you, would you consider showing me the tree?"

I become the reporter on the beat of her small-town police blotter doing her own petty detective work with her pencil tucked under her cap, and finally also the medic, dispatching myself to the scene to cut him down from the tree and to bring him home.

How do I know there was tossing and turning in the bed before? How do I know it was in the middle of the sleepless night and not in the bright gorgeous sunlight of a June day?

How do I know he had his last possessions in an unzipped duffel bag in a corner of the room, the bed unmade, his dinner the night before uneaten, his reading glasses and turquoise ring and three vials of medications left on the bedside table? His one brown shoe dropped to the earth beneath his dangling foot. Two checks from our father in his wallet, $120 apiece.

Here is the incident report, the West Amwell Township police department document, in my hands at last, in front of me. I have opened the envelope—a large manila self-sealer—and I have had to put my head down on my desk, wincing and trying to remember 4-4-4-4 square breathing, every few moments while reading it through.

This is how I know. This is how I know that it was not courageous. That it was not clever or aesthetic or fated.

This is how I know it was 13:40 in the afternoon, military time, when the call came in to dispatch.

The brilliant defensive brain, intuitively, won't read further. Sends my eyes back to the already-read sentences— stalling, stalling, stalling—putting off even for a few seconds what she knows will be up ahead in the report, rereads the first paragraph, fixates on the information there.

That the bed was unmade.

That his belongings were in a green duffel.

That his reading glasses and some medications were on the bedside table.

That in his wallet were two checks from our father.

That the room was a basement extra room used for storage.

Here is the aluminum ladder.

The white plastic electrical cord with multiprong outlets.

The one brown sandal fallen to the dirt beneath his hanging body, his one arm held in rigor straight out to his side.

At 16:36 hours, at 17:01 hours.

A detective arrived, at 17:46 hours, and took photographs of the scene.

The scene is no longer imagined; I've now driven to the property at that address and parked in the overgrown grass. I've peered into the windows, placed my hand on the doorknob, and tried to summon the courage to jiggle open the door, but I've never entered. I remain outside. I see a can of 4C breadcrumbs on the kitchen windowsill.

Where did it happen? What did it look like? Now I know.

Which tree? The one I imagined with its neon yellow canopy? The one I'd have wished for on our mother's densely wooded acres in Vermont if she'd said Yes instead of No? The actual one right here off of Brunswick Pike?

I have privately wondered if it would have been a significantly nicer death for Jeffrey if he had done his last night on Earth's tossing and turning in his mother's custody. Would it have been less anguished to have walked out back and hanged himself from a beautiful tree on his mother's land in Vermont rather than having sat in solitary torpor, on some spare cot, in the basement storage area of some people he didn't know and hung himself from some shitty tree in some New Jersey backyard?

Would it have been nicer for him if, when grasped by the suicidal drive in the middle of the sleepless night, he could have whispered up the stairs on his way out, at the last minute, "Hey, Mom? Ummm, could you come down for a sec?"

If she'd said Yes instead of No when he called to ask if he could come and stay with her for a bit, would he simply have had a nicer death? Still anguished, still inconsolable, but, perhaps, less alone. Less unaccompanied. Less *You are on your own, Buck-o!* Something more *'Night, Mother.*

As if. As if there was such a thing as a *nicer* suicide death. Nicer for whom? My imagination runs wild and is not to be taken seriously. As if it were even possible to be the mother who comes downstairs in the morning to find her son hanging from a rafter and feel some sliver of relief that at least he had been, in a way, Home. As if anywhere else but in your own wild imagination could a parent's familiar home, with the windup clock of your long-ago childhood, and the wooden salt bowl next to the stove, and even the wooden spoons still neatly stashed in their old familiar crock forty years later, have softened the blow, acted as some kind of mollifier, an equivalent to the palliative care that similarly terminal people receive, as if it might have acted as a little dose of morphine to take the edge off as you are walking out the side door, with your aluminum ladder and electrical cord, at the time you are convinced that it's necessary to kill yourself. As if there were home remedies, folk medicines, or DIY hospice for suicidals! This is my obsessive mind on the loose.

I've been confusing my lack of data for the aching vacancy of its meaning, and now, finally, I know. Or, I've known all along but somehow needed these facts: It wasn't funny. It wasn't brave. It wasn't aesthetic. It was not courageous.

The medical examiner, when he receives Jeffrey, finds his toes blue, with his tongue protruding through his teeth. There are fly eggs in his eye sockets and nostrils, and in his scrotum.

CAUSE OF DEATH: ASPHYXIA BY HANGING
MANNER OF DEATH: SUICIDE

I HAD NEVER read an autopsy report before. They examine each of the systems. The cardiovascular, the respiratory, the gastrointestinal, the hematopoietic, the endocrine, the urinary, the musculoskeletal, the neurological.

He begins with a protocol report.

"The decedent is a Caucasian male. His height is 180 cm and weight is 90 kilograms. The decedent has gray-sandy hair. Fly eggs are present over the face and in the ears. The decedent is wearing a blue T-shirt, blue jean shorts. Brown belt and brown moccasin shoes. Toes are blue." I know from the police report that one of his brown shoes had fallen to the dirt beneath him when he was hanging, one shoe on one shoe off, so I have to imagine the moment when the police officer or the medic who cut him down and brought him in stopped and picked up his other shoe. The coroner says "shoes," plural, so the one brown shoe left in the dirt beneath him somehow made its way into the ambulance and then to the morgue. I am moved by this detail; the medic is not about to leave a shoe behind; the medic knows that a pair of shoes is a pair and must remain together.

The coroner has an occasional verbal tic in the transcript of his spoken notes, wherein he doesn't use the article "the" to start certain sentences throughout the examination. "Toes are blue," he declares, as if everybody's toes are blue. Many full sentences but a few shot here and there with no opening articles. Later, he says, "Bones are unremarkable." I smirk reading this and think, *Well, we would like you to believe otherwise!*

"Teeth are present in the maxilla and mandible with tongue protruding through the teeth." Jeffrey is making the face we all make when we are playing, charading, mimicking the dead or dying, where you take your own hands and grasp your own neck and roll your eyes up to show only the whites and you stick your tongue out through your teeth to show that you are croaking, except he is here now actually croaked. The decedent. With his tongue protruding through his teeth.

"A small triangular abrasion is present where the plug was present on the cord.

"Otherwise, the chest is flat. The penis is circumcised and fly eggs are present on the penis and scrotum. The decedent is not wearing underwear."

This. Jeffrey goes commando to his death. Because he always went so, not because he ran out of clean. Not because he didn't care that day. But because Jeffrey went his entire life— except when he was nineteen living with the pygmies and wore a loincloth—commando. I know very little about this brother. But I know that he never wore underpants.

"The back is unremarkable. There are fly eggs present between the gluteus."

And then he rolls Jeffrey back over, after the discovery of the fly eggs in his ass cheeks, and starts to cut him open. The examiner—Dr. Diamonds—in his report clinically performs a "standard y-shaped incision," but me, reading that report, I *roll him over and cut him open.*

My father, in his seventies, asked to schedule regular writing appointments with me to go over how I would write his obituary. He arrived at each meeting with a long list of his accomplishments, handwritten in his black felt pen, and during the hour he would repeatedly insist, "Use *dead*." "Say I *died*." "Don't pussyfoot around with it, okay? I'm not *deceased*. And I haven't *passed away*," he said derisively, with an affected lilt. "I'm just dead, okay?"

"Okay, Dad."

So of course I roll Jeffrey over and cut him open in my mind's eye, reading that coroner's report. We don't *pussyfoot around* with this "standard Y-shaped incision" kind of thing.

One of the least digestible facets of suicide—I mean this kind of suicide: the shower stall danglers, the bridge leapers and eighth-story-window jumpers, oncoming-train track divers; not the fall asleep in the bathtub on a tummy full of pills types—is that the person has to destroy their own body, purposefully, while they are still living in it. He did not *pass away*.

Here is your brother hanging from a tree with an electrical cord around his neck, his one brown sandal fallen to the ground beneath him.

Your father says, "Well. That's over." Your anonymous neighbor says, "Does it come as any surprise?"

But you, privately, with your head down and gulping for breath, you comb and comb and comb the examiner's findings, wondering where those sorts of honesties will be lodged. Where do they find the debris lodged from when your father says about the death of his own son, "Well, if you have to lose one, at least it's the one you liked least"? Under which of the six systems will that be discovered by the county examiner?

I AM REMINDED that the remarkable body has some mechanisms in place for all of the events it will endure, including the event of its own death. I remember this from pregnancy. Even the physical mindset is prepared, the crisp and devout sense of purpose, the unbidden yet faithful arrival and occupation of your regular everyday body by a distinctly new state of being.

Just as in birth and pregnancy, when the joints liquefy and the cartilage goes soft to accommodate the coming event, just as with illness and fever, when there are viruses and invaders, assailants, just as with the dilation of pupils when the lover approaches, the shallow breathing when there are dangers, the magnificent body prepares for death. I hope it was this way for Jeffrey, too. Many people who work in hospice have said so— the dying are bodily prepared for their dying. The body the body the body. The brilliant and beautifully equipped body.

I AM LOOKING for signs that this other state of being came over him in the final hours and hoping that it arrived to protect him from the harshness of what is just up ahead.

Dr. Diamonds has his hands so deep into this body that he notices vegetables and teeth and tiny rents of mesh, but what I wish the medical examiner could report was whether or not there have been tears. I wish there was a seventh system, the lachrymal system, and that he would have to have checked according to his protocol and reported his findings. Were there tears on my brother's cheeks, his nose, his blue T-shirt when they brought him in? I think I would recognize courage if he had zipped his duffel, made his bed, taken his hat with him. If he had gotten properly dressed, procured some sturdy braided rope, a fine worn leather strap, and not grabbed the nearest shitty white plastic electrical extension cord running along the baseboard by the bookshelf. Were there tears, Dr. Diamond?

EVERYBODY TRIED A LITTLE. It's not clean to say Nobody Took Enough Care. Everybody tried to take a little care. And it's also not as clean as "He just courageously decided to put an end to his anguish," either. Not as fatalistically predetermined as "Well, that's over" seems to suggest. Not as simple as "And she said No." Not as linear as "And we blew it to smithereens." Not as direct as "He didn't pay rent for eight years, so I had to ask him to go." But also, not as clean, for those of us who obsessively clean things, as "Cause of Death: Asphyxiation by hanging. Manner of Death: Suicide." Is there not some streak of negligent manslaughter in there, too?

We all tried. He was hard to help. Difficult to persuade or argue with. His eccentricities calcified into manias as he got older, smoked more pot, drank more wine, tried to manage his own moods, as he brewed like a tea bag to a rough and tannic liquid, oversteeped in his own untended psyche. Left to his own devices to solve his own problems, and in our case, in our family, our devices are often extreme Individualism, Exceptionalism, Independence, Contrariness, Self-Reliance, strong cocktails and hard physical work and big laughs. Everybody else goes to see a therapist, a doctor, toughs out the first twenty-eight days of rehab, takes their medicine, humbly recognizes their own vulnerabilities and ordinariness, seeks counsel, gathers in groups of mutual support, but we Hamiltons read books and go for long walks. We find drama entertaining and charming. Consider suffering a sign of weakness. And despair, at least our own, we find self-indulgent. Obviously, we have never once called out sick from work.

We scrupulously only use Dickensian reference points by which to benchmark our own complaints:

We were not orphans, after all, made to sleep on a bed of rags under the kitchen sink, to beg food on the cobblestoned streets. We strictly size up only against the bleakest current political events and tabloid headlines or the pulpy fiction section of the drugstore; and finding that we most certainly did not have live cigarettes extinguished into our bare forearms during cruel games of chicken played out by some psychotic ex-marine father, and that we were not children conscripted into war, traversing the mountains of Afghanistan in the winter in flip-flops, shouldering bazookas, nor marched through the Sudanese jungle and made to machete our neighbors, and knowing that we were not emaciated ribbed children starved in an attic, we deem ourselves extraordinarily sound and hale and lucky and fit and with nothing to complain of, to attend to, and nothing we might need any help with—*don't be ridiculous*, as our mother has eternally commanded—and whatever may have dogged us, chased our minds, or sunk its teeth into our heels we have learned to dismiss, frowning cruelly at our overdramatic selves: *Oh, please. Don't be such a fucking pussy.*

Part Five

COMPLICATED

MY DAD COMES to be known in his circles as a philanthropist. It's mentioned in his obituary. I find myself chuckling about this a little on my drive out to his memorial service, going over the memories of his precarious finances when we were growing up—the countless times he needed to borrow a twenty-dollar bill, the semesters we had been administratively withdrawn from our schools, siphoning gas for the car, the electricity being shut off, robbing Peter to pay Paul. I park outside the building—the service is being held in a renovated industrial brick mill that now houses architectural artifacts. I've come alone. There's a rumor that my sister has threatened to post a cop at the door should I try to attend my dad's service, and I considered bringing my children and my new wife with me, as shield and armor. But I decided in the end to come alone. What will the cop say when he turns me away? *This is a private event for family and friends only?*

Deep breath—no cop—I head in. There is a woman who approaches me immediately. She introduces herself—"Hi, Gabby. It's Deb." I remember her from almost thirty years ago, when I worked one summer at my dad's restaurant, and she would eat solo at the counter. She had a habit of smoking those long skinny brown cigarettes, her eyes watery when she drank her wine. There is a lot of emotional signaling from her; I scan her face wildly, my pupils must be going popcorn crazy trying to read all that she is broadcasting; there is a great deal to decipher and to decode from both her tone and the expression in her eyes:

You are a disappointment
I am a hero
You are a bad daughter
I am a good woman
You did nothing
I did everything

I joke to myself that it's like speed-reading the *Merck Manual: A Desktop Companion to Clinical Diagnoses* just saying hello to this woman, but I am glad to be cornered immediately by her. It gives me a moment to scan the room, to locate my sister out of the corner of my eye and to keep myself positioned accordingly. To notice that Simon has decided not to fly in for this, to nod at Michael across the room. He will soon have a new wife, too, and we are still friendly, like family, and still recognized as uncomfortable figures in the town. We have agreed beforehand not to stir things up by arriving together to this thing, but we have both shown up. I do the best I can. I beam my high beams onto gloomy Deb, with willful exuberance, and I say, "Oh hello! Yes! Of course! Hello hello hello!" She responds with dead eyes, dry and matte.

"I took care of your father every day. I helped him every day. I took care of him. I took him out. I helped your father. I saw your father every day."

Me, all sparkles, glitter, high beams, warm blood, pounding heart; I'm trying to lead with what I wish to receive, to live my aesthetics, to be my charismatic father's daughter, holding her one hand in both of mine.

"Wow. Oh man. Thank you so much. That's so incredible of you!"

She had made her way across the crowded room to be certain to tell me what she had done.

What she had been doing with her life and her time.

All of the very exact things that I had not been doing with mine.

I DID NOT, after all, come back to life as he had hoped. I periodically heard but ignored various reports about his deteriorating condition. The triple bypass surgery. Then the amputation of the foot. The stent finally placed in his groin. Then, when the groin stent and the foot and the open-heart surgery weren't enough, I heard they went back for the rest of the leg to the knee.

Instead, I stayed "up in New York," as the locals say, and began the long arduous work of becoming conscious, conscientious, and self-knowing, taking exceptional pains to hurt no one, and to keep myself out of harm's way. I never came back to life for my father. But I recuperated my relationship with my own son, I eased the rancor from my divorce, I broke up with Michael, I stayed out of sassy trouble and away from colorful stories. I remarried. Only once at the very last minute, I'd gotten a voice message from Simon that our dad had been moved to hospice with only a few hours expected to be left for him, and I felt the sudden urge to palm my dad a five-dollar bill, a strong sudden wish to slip him a little something to have in his pocket as he made that last great journey from Here to There. I quickly called and left him a brief message on his voicemail: "You did great, Dad. You really did great. I hope they are treating you right and keeping you comfortable. You deserve it." And I hung up.

THE MAYOR MADE his way across the room and came to greet me. He looked fixedly down into my face, like a school principal busting the kid who has graffitied the bathroom mirrors, but he was also looking a little afraid, like the kid might have a knife. "He was a complicated man, Gabs, aren't we all?"

"He really was, and we all really are!" I laugh. I want to let the mayor know I haven't lost my sense of humor, so he can see how light of heart, and free of accusation, I am. It's a cheap old trick, I know, but I like to use the Elmer Fudd voice to lighten things up. "A *tewwible pawent,* though." I get the mayor to giggle. Reassuring him that yes, indeed it is true, we are all complicated guys.

I don't want anyone to be concerned about me. I don't want anyone to know that I have been looking too long and too hard at the craggy blue ink on the graph paper—the EKG scan of my own fractured family—trying to understand how the spikes and the plummets add up, how the children keep dying before the parents, how the ignored earliest dark spots have become masses that have metastasized. I'd like to reassure the mayor that it has not been me humorlessly combing through the death certificates of her two older brothers, not me obsessively poring over their obituaries, not me perseverating accusatorially over the strange fact of my siblings dropping dead while my parents whistle along with the classical music station and go to their dance lessons. Not me, paranoid, thinking, *They're winning. We're losing.* As if to be a member of your own family was to be in a high-stakes competition of an extreme sport. I am relieved to be able to reassure the mayor that people are complicated.

Suddenly across the room there is a joyful commotion—the Mummers have come from Philadelphia and are honking their brass in their funny sequined costumes, and everyone is laughing and clapping. Some folks who think I have some celebrity by the little bit of television I have done take this opportunity—there is a huge mood shift in the room, it's time to party!—to ask to have selfies taken with me. I giggle because I am appalled—who has the gall to ask for a selfie with you at a parent's memorial?—and I silently say to my father, in my head, *You reap what you sow, Daddy-o!* But I agreeably stand in front of the daffodils with the star fuckers and beam big smiles. I have arrived to do the best I can and to come in from the cold to be in the company of others who knew this man. He was, in fact, a complicated guy and it feels good to be in a roomful of complicated people.

But the mayor continues, insistent, leaning in close, not letting me move away, so urgently does he need me to agree with him about my father's garden-variety "complexity." It starts to feel like a coercion. His use of the rhetorical "aren't we all," which begs one to return an affirmative answer—*yes, absolutely, aren't we all.*

I start to feel like he is a prosecutor tampering with the evidence of my own experience. He seems like he needs to win a verdict. And anything more damning than "complicated" he will find objectionable. I understand; some people cannot bear even a grain of friction.

Here's the thing, though: I think I could pull "complicated" out of a lineup if they hauled me down to the station. I think I am able to recognize magical, charming, problematic, talented, compelling, corrosive, poisonous, arrogant, mercurial, insecure, unprocessed, out of bounds, generous, romantic, weak, fearsome. I don't wish to overstate my powers of observation or to say that my own research is conclusive, just to say when they ask you to go down to the station and take a look through the two-way mirror, I think I can tell the difference between the regular complicated guy on the left and, on the right, the mythological Saturn eating his children one by one lest they surpass him. That I can pick up the faint but distinct hint of his pleasure while he is chewing through the bones and savoring the juices. "Oh yeah, Gabs, that's been going on for a while."

A family is not taken down in one weekend, by a rare and massive stroke. A whole family is not felled in one night's manic impulse to take itself out to the nearest branch and hang itself. It dies in a slow and almost imperceptible way, as if an odorless gas, like carbon dioxide, has been seeping into the house undetected for hours and hours. And it will leave them sprawled on the floor, one by one, cut down in the middle of their mundane activities, tying the laces on their soccer cleats, stirring something simmering on the stove with a wooden spoon. It takes a long time for a boat to sink.

But this is a day for celebration, and I wish to reassure the mayor that I am not here to vandalize, that, indeed, I am here for the party. I wish the mayor to know that I am big big big on clemency.

But you can't get there on the mayor's insistence, can't instantly take to the common wisdom so blithely dispensed: *Let it go! Lighten up! People are complicated!* You will eventually get there, but this is a long, intricate story with a punch line that will need to be fumbled a few times first in the early retellings. *Oh, wait! I forgot the most important detail! With your permission, may I start again?* as my dad used to say, when setting up one of his new numbers. And he would go back over it, tell it again, and finally land the joke. This takes quite a few first drafts in which your father is not quite so agreeably or benignly complicated, and in which he is more, frankly, lethally so. For those first several drafts you are still deep in the stage of discovery, observing that actual lives are at stake. You are still preparing the slides, slipping them under the microscope, analyzing the squigglings.

Brothers beating brothers.

Sisters fucking over sisters.

Daughters clicking phones.

Everybody always throwing their car into reverse and peeling out.

Fire on top; dead from the waist down.

We turned and inflicted on one another what we each had endured alone.

But it's true that eventually, after you mourn what is rightfully yours to mourn, after you ask yourself to accept the full brunt of the solemn truth, a new kind of vitality arrives. The kind where you are not in a drawer at the morgue, you are not in an urn of ashes, you are not starting your day with a one-hitter of walloping hashish, you are instead at the memorial party collegially giggling with the mayor about what a complicated guy your father was while the Mummers in their sequined suits play saxophones and march through the room. Among the hundred or so people who have gathered, I meet his tap dancing instructor—a woman delighted by my father and his indomitable spirit.

"Did you find it quite moving?" I ask and she says that yes, she did.

I confirm for her the inherent poignancy of it—an eighty-six-year-old man with one of his legs amputated due to complications from diabetes, his two sons buried before him, a stent in each chamber of his heart under two consecutive surgeries—and still, "came to tap dance classes and never gave up!" she tells me.

In some contexts, tap dancing with one leg is beautiful, a signal of an indomitable spirit. She is moved by the pluck of the dashing old devil in the wheelchair, getting around with the help of a prosthetic leg, and still managing a forty-five-minute tap dance class.

To the unknowing—all fire looks like glitter. All branches grow straight.

But to me, like Jeffrey's insistence on the nuanced distinction between ash and apple branches, to me, our father's energy to stay alive just a little longer seemed less a thing of glittering beauty and more as if he were still campaigning for a profile in *The New York Times*.

⁂

HE DID HAVE an indomitable streak, and his grip on life was indeed ferocious but strangely not, it seemed to me, in order to grab the great pleasures one last time. He was not clinging to the doorframe

for one more deep inhale of a pint of freshly ground coffee beans,

for the eye-watering burn of the ammoniated chicken manure in the henhouse,

to hear one last time the howl of the lonely dogs at night's edge,

for the scratch of the branches on the roof,

to look up from his desk to find the two squirrels roughhousing in the crotch of the tree outside his window.

He was not lashing his fingers to the last of his days to hear the onions sizzle in their duck fat,

to listen to his daughters' voices,

to call everyone close in order to finally say what needed to be said.

But that's me. For all the ways he is me and I am him, these were not his pleasures. He is not the type who thrills to have caught a glimpse of his ten-year-old boy preparing for his first day of fifth grade, his clothes laid out the night before,

alone in the bathroom with the mirrored cabinet doors open for a three-way view, the shampoo *and* the conditioner,

the wide-toothed comb,

testing the choices of deodorant first on the back side of his knees to see if he will like it under his arms.

He is not the kind who would beg to live one more day if only for one last chance to stand stick-still in the hall, to spy through the crack in the door left ajar, to notice on which side the boy finally decided to part his hair.

He is not one to quietly show up in the auditorium on time and to wait with all the other regular parents for our children to finish their difficult high school entrance test. It is not him whose heart explodes as—two by three then by the hundred—the parents start clapping, as each gangly, awkward child files into the gym after the three-hour exam to get into a specialized high school. Over the loudspeaker, the proctor says, "These guys just took a really big test!" And then the room is thunder itself, the parents raining their admiration down onto children we don't even know, but whose plight we can recognize. He is not Me.

I STAND IN the room of my father's memorial until the end—the Mummers have left, the mayor has moved on, I have a glass of wine, and people, strangers all of them, come up and introduce themselves to me. These are not my father's intimates, these are people who knew him at his restaurant, whose tables he has stopped by, whose houses he has designed, and they tell me about all the causes my father donated his time to, all the money he helped them raise, the design work he so generously offered pro bono, the support and encouragement he regularly showered upon them, the pinches they were in that my father rescued them from, and they are all effusive, positive and radiant about my dad; and I nod *yes, yes, a philanthropist, generous beyond belief,* and confirm for them what they tell me they experienced. I recognize it as true.

I take the back roads as I am leaving, just as dusk is settling in. I drive north on the winding county road, past cornfields and horse farms, and as I come around a bend in the road past a stand of trees, there, a sudden flash of two mirror orbs staring at me, a deer frozen at the bank. And in the stubbly field behind him, six others, still as statues.

A BLESSING

M Y MOTHER IS eighty-seven years old when I see her again, fourteen years since the last time I saw her with my infant son and Italian husband. My wife is coincidentally from a town in New Hampshire just over an hour from where my mother lives across the Vermont border. We have rented a summer vacation property for a week. There's been a lot of jumping off the dock into the lake, ping-pong on the screened-in porch during cocktail hour, blueberry muffins baked with local blueberries, family dinners that linger long after sundown, and when one of the loons calls lonesomely across the lake we all hush our conversation, tap one another on the arm to *ssshh* for a second so we can hear the aching, haunting echo.

My boys love diving off the dock, being dragged behind the speedboat on inner tubes while Ashley's dad floors the gas pedal, after-dinner glow stick tag at night on the front sloping lawn. But wandering around in the huge old creaking wooden house we've rented that has insects and cobwebs and locked closet doors and dark staircases that go nowhere has taken some getting used to. The boys have ended up sharing a room even though there is plenty of space to spread out, and I often find them in the morning passed out in the same bed, the laptop between them, some movie or television series going with the volume off but the subtitles up. It's their version of the old-fashioned night-light we used when they were little and had to find the bathroom in the middle of the night.

Meanwhile, it's undeniable: the palpable fact of my mother's exceeding Nearbyness. All week it has been skittering around in my mind, a darting thought here and there during the quiet at the end of the day: *Should we go visit her?* Even the kids are curious about this woman they have never met or don't remember meeting, and they say an hour in the car each way won't kill them. We discuss it as just another possible activity, like going to the local waterfall, a nearby miniature golf course, the pick-your-own-berries farm. For me, the proximity is too tempting to pass up: I kind of want to know what she looks like. She must be an old woman by now.

The first thing I realize is that in just the couple of years that have passed since I last called her, she can't hear me over the phone. I have to speak exceedingly slowly, enunciating, articulating, and repeating—which is in some ways no different than how it has always been with her, a continuation of her usual confusion around the telephone—but it seems things have devolved; it takes quite a bit of work to get her to understand what I am proposing.

"You live in New Hampshire?" she asks, surprised.

A visit?

To Vermont?

For lunch?

"Oh, of course I'd like that," she says, laughing. "Wait a minute, Gabri, and let me use my good ear!" She pretends to switch the phone to the other side. "Oh, that's better," she laughs again, now that I have repeated my suggestion for the fourth time. It's one part schtick and three parts actual hearing loss. Once she can hear what's being said, her mind is still sharp enough to get it. And her humor is very intact.

It turns out to be an easy and beautiful drive. When we arrive, I'm glad to have brought the whole crew—the kids, the wife, the dog—and I like the way they decoy, giving me lavish time to look her over, myself unnoticed as she tries so hard to take inventory of all these people in front of her, whom she is now meeting for the first time. I take advantage of the minutes it takes for Marco and Leone to repeat themselves as she stares at their faces, turns her good ear to their mouths but also keeps her eyes on their lips, as she admires the family resemblance in the boys, looks for recognizable traits. But she is not so slow or so old that she has lost her bite; while she is busy looking them over she is also bitching about the dog.

"Ah, no!"

"Not in the house!"

"Get that animal out of my house!"

Ashley takes the dog outside and my mother yells after her—"And not in my garden, either!"

I stand over her by more than a foot, and it is disorienting, looking down into my mother's upturned face. A position we have never found ourselves in. It's just choreography, stage blocking—who sits where, who exits left, who enters upstage right—but the view has a physical impact. I find myself in a very good mood; I am made careful, gentle, just by the new vantage point.

Her skin is impeccable, and I am interested to see this for my own future. Her teeth, however, are a disaster. I at first think she has been eating toffee candies but now I see that most of her teeth are missing. Broken in half. The few that are left are tarred over. She has some bright white ill-fitting falsies on top that are incongruously beautiful, and they are not held in securely, so she slurs a little as her denture slips around. The denture is just a bridge, not a full set, it gives her some frontals for the purpose of dignity and vanity. I make a note in my head to visit the orthodontist as soon as we return to the city. Her face and head and ears and nose are giant—a prize cauliflower at the state fair—while her wrists and neck and ankles are as slim as sticks. She is so tiny. Yet still sturdy as a broom handle, and thick in the waist.

I stand over her, inspecting her, scanning her—and inventorying my own response to her—with metal-detector-static urgency.

And it turns out, metallurgically speaking, there is no buzz. Everything is quiet. I am immediately aware of my Goliath strength, my skyscraper height. I could snap her wrist with my one hand. Her frailty, like her size, makes me take extra care, to step extra cautiously and go very slowly. No sudden moves. When you find yourself with that kind of advantage you must never unleash it.

My wife says after we leave, "I had no idea she'd be so small."

Does every new spouse say this once they meet the colossal figure who is not their own mother, not their own mythology?

Her teeth were not as sharp as I thought they would be. Her ears were not as furry as I expected.

It's invisible, it's private, what the father hisses to his son through clenched teeth before turning in to the crowded room with his captivating, lucid smile, beginning the setup to his newest joke. What the furious wife spits out—"You're late"—to her arriving husband before turning her dazzling charm on for the waiter: "I'd love a glass of sparkling, please." It's the horrid prerogative of intimacy. Do we think we will arrive at the homes of our mothers whom we have been explaining to our wives and children for decades and expect to find the attic room strewn with chains and padlocks, the bed of rags under the kitchen cabinet? Do we imagine there will be a seven-foot-tall figure in long black tattered robes who creaks open the heavy wooden door and greets us with her one ghoulishly long and bony finger?

She's tiny. With broken teeth. Her thin white hair is combed and pinned neatly. She has done her eye makeup as she has done it every day: a greenish-brown eyeliner, dark brown mascara, and we find her, as ever, in her apron, disapproving of the dog.

She is done looking at my boys, and she wants to show us around. She shows us to her bedroom now that she has moved down to the ground floor and stops to show the boys her father's diploma from the music conservatory in France, dated September 3, 1894, and framed on the wall. "This is your great-grandfather's diploma," she points out to them, as they stare at it and then at her. She points out that the wide wooden steps to her upstairs bedroom have become *a risk she doesn't need to tempt,* she says, so she sleeps now, she wants to show us, in the guest room on the ground floor. I am shocked to discover she sleeps in the very bed I slept in as a child. The same mattress, the same box spring. She has never thrown anything away. My chest of drawers that had been in my childhood room, now hers. It had been blue, then a kind of muddy brick red. You can see both paint jobs, one bleeding through the other, mine the cornflower glossy blue and then hers, the muddy brick autumn red.

And there it is, then: The Blanket. I see it folded neatly on the footstool of her reading chair and I go to it immediately.

"Oh my god! Here is the blanket!"

I pick it up and unfold it in front of everyone. "Holy shit! Here it is. My blanket. The blanket!" My black fake-fur blanket. With its brown velour trim—as narrow and long as a standard bath towel. Exactly the size of a bath towel.

Everybody understands except for her. I have told my kids this story; everybody in my own family, the one I have made here with this group, this wife, these sons, this pooch—they know what I am referring to. And they are smiling like factcheckers who have rounded up the facts and discovered that the story squares up. *The writer says there was a blanket, and here it finally is.* But my mother doesn't understand the commotion. Her eyes are lit up, and she is smiling at our smiling, excited by our excitement, but she hasn't any idea what it's about. She is pleasantly bewildered. I briefly try and explain it to her, in a rush—

"Oh, Mom, it's a long story, my story with this blanket, and Dad asking for a blanket, and you not letting him have one and the creaking of that big wicker chest at the bottom of your stairs that woke you up . . ."

I go on in bright singsong run-on fragments—she doesn't

understand a thing I am saying, and possibly also can't quite hear me, she is so focused on my face, my mouth. I wonder if she reads lips to help with her hearing, or perhaps she just doesn't remember this incident—*perhaps selectively!*—but she lights up at the mention of the wicker chest and points to it there, in the corner of the room. The old wicker chest with brass hinges and front latches that incomprehensibly only comes up to my thighs but, the last time I saw it, came up to my armpits.

"There it is right there!" She proudly gestures. Her face is all big grins and happy eyes—she is proud of her thrift, and she is remarking on how amazing she is that she still uses the wicker hamper this many decades later. That she is not the kind of person who disposes of perfectly good and perfectly useful things. For her this is the most important detail. I, meanwhile, am trying to describe to her the cruelest cruelty she has ever performed.

And then there he is. Jeffrey. In a squat cardboard box, on top of the dresser. She has placed an index card on the box of ashes; in her handwriting, she has written,

"This premature death is a blessing in that it terminates at the right time a life of uncertainty and of spiritual misery."

Atop the box of his ashes she has placed a very handsome photo of him, taken when he must have been around thirty years old. He is still young enough in the photo to have his very good looks: His strong nose and his full lips and his thick eyebrows and his wide-brimmed straw hat and his cotton shirt. His clear, intelligent eyes.

As we linger in front of the dresser with Jeffrey's ashes in the box there, she says, in her cheerful sweet baby voice, "And you know, Gabri, I kiss him every morning when I wake up, and I kiss him every night when I go to sleep! My little Jeffrey." In her li'l baby voice she tells us what she tells him: "Good morning, precious boy!" Every morning and every night before bed, she stops at the dresser and gives his ashes her warmth and affection, her devotion and tenderness.

HOUDINI

AND THEN, FINALLY, four years since we all drove away
and left her there that summer, there is the phone call
I've always known was coming. This time, it's from Simon. In
the dead of winter. She has fallen.

Our mother has fallen at ninety years old and fractured her
pelvis. Simon has already driven across country, has already
been taking care of her for over a month. He has put her in the
hospital, and he doesn't come out and say it, but he is clearly
now going out of his gourd; he's stir-crazy, claustrophobic,
antsy, itchy, caged in. It's been a stressful, long, dark Decem-
ber spent in her mountaintop house, alone on fifty-eight acres,
away from his own work and his own life and his affectionate
wife back in sunny Santa Barbara, California. I have heard
that possibly he and my sister are on the outs, as they sometimes have been over the decades, and that they, too, are not
speaking. He has been at my mother's doing everything with

no help, on his own. And he is now trying to pitch me on the idea, in the middle of January, of coming to relieve him, while our mother remains bedridden in the nursing home, deteriorating. I'd wondered about her every once in a while, over the past four years since last I saw her on her mountaintop, scolding my dog. "She's gonna live to be a hundred, I bet. She's a beast!" I'd chuckled during those years, a little proudly, as if it reflected well on me and predicted my own longevity. But here was Simon calling to tell me, already more than a month after the fact, that she'd fallen and had been bedridden ever since. She is clearly not going to make it to a hundred.

I am unexpectedly available, in both pragmatic and emotional capacities, to relieve him—there's a pandemic across the world that has stopped life as we know it, my restaurant is shuttered, my children are hardly children anymore, they are young adults, and I have, after decades of working on it, become increasingly psychologically "organized." But, more persuasively, I immediately understand that Simon, though he would never admit it, is suffering. I can hear it in his voice, which is overly good-natured and casual and exaggeratedly indifferent. I have to think that if Simon is calling me, of all people, Simon who can get himself out of any jam, any locked room, any predicament that he finds himself in—Houdini-like—that if he is calling me, the sister he doesn't have a relationship with, the daughter who has been cut out of all the wills and universally denounced—then he must be in an impossibly tight corner. He does what we all do; he pretends he is rich with options and acts like he could take it or leave it—the promise of my relief. He tries to spin it as an opportunity for me that he is generously offering. "Maybe you'd like a nice little mountain getaway, Gabs," he suggests, like he's fencing hot watches to some rube on Canal Street. "Simon. Stop. I said I'll do it," I say. It seems impossible for him to know anything about me, so I imagine he will never know that I feel an instant and crystal urgency to protect him. "Sime, I need half a week to tie some things up here and then I'll be up. I'll be there."

And here she is at the nursing home facility that accepts Medicaid. In what I call her "shower stall"—half of a room with a beige plastic shower curtain drawn between her and the lady in the next bed, also ninety.

Now I am the one standing at the bedside, a hundred feet tall, a voice that can set off car alarms, that can be heard all the way down the hall at the nurses' station should I call, and she is lying prone, toothless, a fracture at the pelvis, her wrists and ankles as thin as crackers. I am able to do the job that needs to be done here, and it feels uncomplicated. We have passed each other in that long corridor, brushed elbows, she is coming off of her shift, and now I am punching in on the clock. Ready to start the work. And it's a very simple job: Small, fragile creatures must be held warmly and thoughtfully looked after. No other thing is on the schedule. This is not the time to go over some of your complaints. To finish up any business.

"Gabri, what are you doing here?" she asks with gratitude and surprise after I find my way down the fluorescent hall and come around the corner into her room. "How nice of you to come all this way to see me!"

ONCE WHEN WE are little, we pass on the highway a three-car wreck, spiderweb windshields, crinkle-cut front ends, ambulances galore, and she says into the thick, terrible silence

that fell upon us all as we stared, as we slowed to a crawl passing that wreck, "There are no such things as accidents, only
carelessness!" as if scolding the dead and the injured. *Tsssk*ing
through her teeth at the severity of what we'd just passed, at
the severe consequences of carelessness.

I see her in the hospital bed, and it is involuntary, immediately obvious what is required. It's as if there is a stray dog
without a collar dangerously zigzagging the highway. You
swerve your car over to the breakdown lane, you reverse, throw
on the hazards, step out of the car, hold open the door, and
take the lost dog into your back seat. You do not scold the
frightened dog. You brush the hair back from your mother's
face with your cool hand.

This is not the time to confront, or to withhold. This is not
the time to point out her misspellings or complain about her
poor posture or criticize the garish outfit she has selected from
the donated Catholic charities box—a lavender sweatshirt
with two glassy-eyed white kittens appliquéd on the front and
fleece pajama pants, an adult diaper, no-slip treaded hospital
socks. If she had been available for that kind of reckoning it
would have had to have been a long, long time ago. She is no
more capable of that now than she was then. She has always,
in a way you now see vividly, she has always been this incapable. She is frail and lost and small, all kinds of small. A child
in a bed. You freely give her the kisses on both cheeks she used
to demand, the ones you usually despise giving her, because she
has always made them last too long and has always taken more
from you than you were comfortable giving. Now, it costs you
nothing to give her what she wants. In fact now, you start to
notice, it gives you something in return. You hope you are not
too flagrant, too smug, too vindictive about it, but you notice

how correct you feel, demonstrating for your mother what it is to do the right thing at the right time to the right degree. You hold her hand. Let her look you over. It has been so long, and her memory has noticeably shortened, she can't believe her eyes. You rub her feet.

"I'm sorry you have to see me this way," she apologizes.

"It must be difficult to see me like this," she repeats. She doesn't understand that this is the first time in your life you have ever seen her surrendered and yielding. The first time in her life that she is unable to rely on herself, and she suddenly is unrecognizable, to herself and to you as well.

You find it the opposite of difficult; it is effortless. It's a captivating and wondrous pleasure. You have heard of so many once-loving, once-tender mothers who, as their senility and dementia set in, became newly monstrous, vicious, vituperative, and in this one miracle of fate, your own usually harsh and acidic mother has gone totally the other way.

She is complimentary, appreciative, thankful.

You get her some fresh water in the plastic cup from the faucet in the attached bathroom, where there is a potty chair over the toilet. "Such a pretty girl," she says, as you return to her bed and hand her the water. "What a nice figure, you've really kept your figure," she admires.

"I'm sorry I'm just not in my right head," she keeps saying. "My brain isn't quite right." And then, because she's retained her enormous sense of humor, she speaks my part for me: "You seem just the same to me!" She laughs and laughs. "Oh, at least we can laugh, Gabri. At least we have that."

I think, perhaps ungenerously: *That's at most what we have, Mom. That's all this family knows how to do, laugh— this family that lacks the courage to admit its sorrows.* But I don't say it. I gently scooch her over a tiny bit in the bed, make a space for myself, and I sit with her and hold her hand and laugh with her. And tell her I'll be back again tomorrow.

The next day she says the same thing when I arrive. "Gabri, what are you doing here?" and I explain the whole thing again, scooting her over in the bed, holding her hand, reminding her of who she is, how she got here, where "here" even is. The body the body the body—again the magnificent body—it has somehow intuitively hastened the dulling of her mind in perfect coalition with her now almost unusable body. A month ago, she was driving her own car, cooking her own meals, buying her own groceries, stacking her own firewood. And now she's here, and alive, but all she can do is slowly and painfully get herself to the toilet—and not always in time—and get herself back into her hospital bed. She sits up for her meals. Fumbles with the buttons on her boom box to make the classical music station stop and start. And spends her days and nights trying to piece it all together in her mind: who she is, where she is, why and how she got here.

I SPEND A day of overlap with Simon when I first arrive, the two of us alone that evening in her house, while he prepares to gather up his things and head back to his home and life in California. I am the relief runner in the relay race, and he is passing me the baton. He tells me to be sure to bring big bags of candy for the nurses. He is now a silver-haired man, a brother I hardly know and with whom I haven't spent twenty-four hours, cumulatively, in forty years. I get dinner going, clean her house a bit, and, as I am sweeping the bathroom floor, a pebble rattles out from under the broom. I bend to pick it up and discover it is one of her teeth, yellowed, dry, chalky. I will take it to her tomorrow, to this now thoroughly defanged creature. I will place it under her pillow and tell her to see what the tooth fairy will bring in the morning. She will smile, revealing her loose white falsies, with the licorice-black cavities in the back.

Simon packs up his van, repairs the broken showerhead, explains to me the piles and piles and piles of her medical papers, her property documents, her insurance files, her utility bills, her correspondence. He tells me to sell her car. All over the dining table, the guest bed, the desk, and the floor are papers. I have satisfactorily completed the highest level of education in my family—I have done all of the reading and all of the writing and have acquired a master's degree; have birthed and managed two children and all of their immunizations and registrations and educations; have employed over a hundred people involving their W-9s and W-2s and their FICA taxes and their disability insurance; have sued and been sued, have formed LLCs and an S-corp; have filed and paid quarterly business taxes and annual personal taxes; have owned pets and tracked their medications; have been married and divorced and married again; have requested and received and compiled dozens of complex and sensitive documents to attain dual Italian and American citizenships for myself and my children, involving FBI background checks and fingerprinting and notarizing and police records from the five different states in which I have had an address in my lifetime; and yet I am looking at those piles of paper that he is walking me through, nearly trembling.

What has this woman, alone on her mountaintop, mostly un-employed, been doing these past thirty years?

We finally sit down to eat the dinner I have cooked, and I discover for the next dinner hour a man with a lifetime's ré-sumé stacked with near-misses, dodged bullets, last-minute escapes, who delights in the retelling, even the stories of the couple of early times he got pinned. He himself is giggling and his eyes are bright with relived excitement as he describes how he escaped, Houdini-like, how he performed his amazing last-minute coups by which he saved his own ass. "You remember Bulgur, right, and his whole deal?" he asks, referring to a fa-mously gropey man from our hometown who we all knew and rather loved and made excuses for, whose predilection for boarding school boys we good-naturedly overlooked. "He al-most got me one night, as I was coming up Mechanic Street, tried to get me to sleep over." He recounts these stories as sporting events, as if his entire life has been one uninterrupted winning streak, not a single upset in over fifty years!

He recounts them, one after the other, as bits of great humor. A twelve-year-old out in the night, figuring out where to sleep. An eleventh-grader hitchhiking the snowy northern highways with not enough money for a train ticket home for winter break. I go along with it during dinner, but I'll never be able to look down, bird's-eye view, at a seventeen-year-old boy on the side of an interstate highway climbing up into the cab of an eighteen-wheeler in the dead of a wintry night and think, *Oh, that IS a funny one!* It may in fact end up being a lively, colorful story of kindness and human generosity and one for the books, but after twenty minutes of these stories, I am up from the table, getting more ice, pouring another gin and tonic. I know what it is to walk yourself to school, to be a teenage cocktail waitress, to find yourself on the side of an interstate highway with not enough cash for a bus ticket.

All through dinner he exuberantly tells this same harrowing story, different nights, different highways, the same story in thirty different exotic flavors, all the near-misses, the barely-escapeds, the close calls, the brushes with frostbite, death, fondling, diddling, and being stranded, *up shit's creek without a paddle.*

There are guys who live to tell big stories about the hunt, the deal, the babelicious babe, the sport, the race, the stock market, the derring-do, but for Simon it is only about the Dodged Bullet. He even has a near-miss story from as recently as the week or maybe the month before—he is not twelve or seventeen or twenty-one or thirty-three—he is a fifty-six-year-old man sitting at our mother's table enjoying roast chicken and braised black lentils and a bitter greens salad. And it's often hard to follow the exact details because he speaks so quickly and elides huge chunks of contextual material. He is not concerned with the webbing and the infrastructure that holds good stories in fact-checkable place. Exactly like our father, he just likes the glittery parts and the explosive punch lines.

Somehow, on his way to Vermont to retrieve his van and check on Mom, he has missed a few connections at the major airports and, in a pinch, has been forced to catch a little puddle-jumper plane from some tiny airfield in New Hampshire, and "Gabs, I'm not kidding, the pilot couldn't navigate the fog, and we nearly lost it in the valley between the mountains!" His eyes are wide and glittering. He is alive.

"Simon, do you ever wonder why you've found yourself so

often in this kind of near-miss situation?" I ask, and he pauses and says, "Whoa! I know, right? It's always like this! It must be my karma!"

I would've taken it a different way, but whoever tells the story is the one who is allowed to define himself; and that's what he thinks: karma.

After dinner, he steps out into the frigid Vermont night, sits on the back bumper of his van, smokes a cigarette; I clear the plates, put the dinner away, handwash the dishes using as little water as possible, finding the same pearly ivory liquid in the bottle on the ledge by the sink where she has always kept it. Before bed, I say:

"It's funny that the two she left behind are the two that have come back to deal with her." And he says:

"You think too much."

A COMEDY. OF ERRORS.

A ND NOW IT'S up to me. I drive up every week, or every other. I bring butterscotch candies for the nurses. I go to visit my mom in her "shower stall"; she's on an eight-to-ten-minute memory loop now, before we have to start again from the exact beginning and repeat everything. I've brought her the tooth I swept up from her bathroom floor. I slip it under her pillow, tell her I'll be back tomorrow to see if the tooth fairy came. She finds this very amusing. Ridiculous even. I tell her I love her, and she rolls her eyes and says, "Okay, if that makes you feel better."

I'm my own Antigone, making sure everybody gets a proper burial, whether they were honorable or not; you can't leave anybody out on the battlefield to be eaten by the vultures. To rot in the sun.

"What are you working on, Gabri? What are you writing these days?" she asks.

I sigh.

"Oh, you know me, Mom, what I do, what I always do, even if it's just some stupid piece about salad dressing or sandwiches it's always the same: I just always write about how much I loved everybody. And, you know. The loss, the destruction, the demise, the decay, the death of my beautiful, potent, promising family. Anyway, just that! The usual. That's what I'm working on." I giggle. Then pause, in a prolonged silence.

"Obviously, it's a comedy," I add.

Now she takes a beat. One moment of silence, this time taken by her. "Of errors," she replies.

AUTHOR'S NOTE

I HAVE CHANGED THE names of some people in this book. I have airbrushed a couple of people out of scenes where they should have existed because they would have distracted from the larger story. I have compressed and contracted time in several instances. And I have condensed recurring, nearly identical events into one for clarity, drive, and momentum. Otherwise, this book is a true account of my experiences as I remember them.

ACKNOWLEDGMENTS

I N   M Y   H O U S E , we refer a little too often to a joke about the writing life . . . borrowed/butchered from Sean Michael Greer's book *Less*. "It's like living alone . . . living alone with a tiger." I'd like to enthusiastically thank and praise and console all of the following people who either had to work with me, work around me, live with me, live without me, wait for me, or wait up for me while I was writing this book. Kim Witherspoon, William Callahan, and all at Inkwell; Pam Cannon, Hilary Redmon, Whitney Frick, and the Random House team; Geoff Bankowski, Al Filreis, Megan Moore, Lawrence Hauser, Heidi Dorow, Russell Salmon, and Julian Fleisher from my cherished civilian circle.

And from the rooftops, I'd like to shout, I love you, Ashley Merriman. Your effortless way with both the "alone" and the "tiger" is a daily perfection.

Peace on Earth.

ABOUT THE AUTHOR

Gabrielle Hamilton is the author of the *New York Times* bestseller *Blood, Bones & Butter,* which won the James Beard Foundation's award for Writing and Literature, and the cookbook *Prune.* She is the chef/owner of Prune restaurant in New York City's East Village. She received an MFA in fiction writing from the University of Michigan, has written a food column for *The New York Times,* and her work has appeared in *The New Yorker, The New York Times, GQ, Bon Appétit, Vogue, The Wall Street Journal, Elle,* and *House Beautiful.* In 2021 she edited *The Best American Food Writing* and her work has been featured in both that publication and in *The Best American Essays.* Hamilton has received four different James Beard Awards and has won an Emmy Award for her role on PBS's *The Mind of a Chef.*